THE NEW
CHRISTIAN ETHICS

Don Cupitt

SCM PRESS LTD

British Library Cataloguing in Publication Data

Cupitt, Don
The new Christian ethics.
1. Christian ethics
I. Title
241

ISBN 0–334–02201–0

First published 1988
by SCM Press Ltd
26–30 Tottenham Road, London N1

Typeset at The Spartan Press Ltd
Lymington, Hants
and printed in Great Britain by
Billings and Sons Ltd, Worcester

Contents

Introduction

No subject is more important to us than ethics, and yet everyone who teaches it is uncomfortably aware that no subject has become more boring. Large parts of its historic vocabulary have in recent decades simply died on us, in a way that presents a peculiar challenge to *Christian* ethics, for what has died is precisely a whole series of residually-theological terms, distinctions, images and models. A Christian writer who himself wants to overcome all the received 'theological' ways of thinking is perhaps well placed to attempt a reinvention of ethics in general and Christian ethics in particular.

By a 'theological' way of thinking about ethics I mean something like this: we were brought up to think of the ethical as being like a set of invisible guide-rails (or 'frame', as I shall call it). One's conduct was supposed to be constrained or directed by exalted and invisible entities of rather obscure status.

The vocabularies in which the frame was described were diverse and confusing. It was a lot of values, or obligations. It consisted of traditional pathways that we should walk on, bounds that we should keep within, rules that we should follow, commands and prohibitions that we should obey and respect, goods that we should pursue, or natures to which we should pay due regard.

What was 'theological' was perhaps the combination of a general feeling of the super-importance of the whole subject with a very variegated vocabulary, and also a pervasive dualism which subordinated the actual to something unseen, ideal and compelling. Also theological was the atmosphere of moral realism. The ethical put a special sort of extrinsic pressure on you, so that you had to think of it as objectively and constrainingly *one* and *real*. There was indeed a second-order moral pressure to be a realist, just as there is also in religion and (nowadays) in science. You were not taking the enterprise really seriously unless you were a realist – and in this way the ethical in particular was protected from scrutiny. It was sacred and mysterious, so *Keep your nose out!* Don't pry. Just confess its objective reality.

The purpose of all this mystification was very simple. It was to hide something that would otherwise be blindingly obvious, namely the fact that the frame is merely cultural. We evolved it, and it is still changing. There are alternatives to it, for other cultures, other faiths, other periods have different frames. But because the ethical is indeed more important to us than anything else, it seemed right that its lowly origins should be veiled. It was objectified, made part of the eternal constitution of things, surrounded by an aura of solemnity and made to impinge upon us as if from beyond ourselves. Thus much of moral philosophy remained the ghost of theology until early modern times.

The standard caricature says that in the nineteenth century moral realism (with its doctrine of conscience) and moral*ism* together became peculiarly intense, non-rational and oppressive. If that was so, it was only because they were at the point of collapse. The whole realm of the ethical was being rapidly demythologized by a better understanding of historical change, cultural diversity, human psychology and (above all) the creative, mythmaking and thought-constraining power of society itself. Critical thinking was shining its torch into various dark and neglected corners of the culture, and everywhere the result appeared to be the same: something whose pedigree had hitherto seemed highly exalted turned out after all to have had very humble beginnings. A suspicion grew that morality is very often a figleaf, a deception, a cloak for something else. The moralism of life's winners merely expressed their self-satisfaction. It consolidated their success while disguising the means by which they had achieved it. The moralism of life's losers was a dream of revenge or a rationalization of their defeat. So morality began to get a dirty name. It received a drubbing from the great masters of suspicion, Marx, Nietzsche and Freud, and was thoroughly demystified. In ethical theory the sequel has been various kinds of emotivism, existentialism, pragmatism, Wittgensteinian quietism and neo-naturalism. At a more popular level, it has been the relaxed relativism, the casual nihilism which the old detect with so much dismay in the young.

There have also been great gains. When we grasp that the ethical – just like the law, and like religion – is not sacred and timeless but a mere changing human improvisation, then we become morally responsible in a new way. We are not just responsible for living up to our standards; we are also responsible for our standards themselves. The frame, as we called it, is not sacrosanct any more. It is ours. We bring it into the workshop, examine it and attempt to modify it. We actually set out to redesign our own values, as feminist writers are now trying to do with the man-woman relationship.

This is interesting and puzzling: do we have a second-order morality that we can use to evaluate our first-order morality? How can we subject morality itself to moral criticism? But we *do*, and we need to watch what we are doing.

In relation to all these vitally-important developments Christian ethics is in an unhappy situation. It is historically perhaps the single most important element in our moral tradition, but it cannot make any useful contribution to modern society while it remains so completely imprisoned within precisely those theological and realistic ways of thinking from which ethics in general has struggled free. If it is to join in, Christian ethics must get itself up to date and get on a par with the rest of the culture. It must free itself from the shackles of myth, obscurantism and its traditional state of protected unconsciousness.

I want to put the issue in much stronger terms. For almost a century we have lived *after* truth, *after* virtue and *after* the death of God. No frame is pre-existent and sacrosanct.

All frames – whether we are talking about religion, morality, scientific theory, philosophy, logic or whatever – *all* frames are human historical-cultural improvisations. We made them. We are responsible for them. Their function is – always was – to overcome nihilism by imposing some structure upon and inject-ing some value into our life-world. The big change in the modern world is that society is now very large-scale, very highly diversified, in permanent rapid change and highly reflective. Result: we have become aware of our frames, and we've now got the responsibility for continuously and consciously redesigning them. We may look back nostalgically to the days when design was traditional and traditionally just right, when spade and fork and drystone wall and five-bar gate were already exactly what they should be and did not have to be thought about. But in these days the most everyday articles need to be redesigned, consciously, rather often and on scientific principles. So it is now with, for example, the civil law, and so it is with even our moral values and our religious beliefs. To suppose that there is some compulsory objective and timeless truth in these matters is like supposing that the design of a garden fork copies a heavenly archetype and cannot be altered. We just don't think like that any more.

The upshot of all this is that (contrary to a common complaint) art is becoming more and more central to the culture.[1] We make truth and we make values. The history of a culture is a history of the production of new metaphors and the making of new moral claims. We keep our moral tradition alive by continually inventing new human rights and by discovering ever-new topics of social concern. Our moral tradition now lives like an art tradition, by creation and criticism. There was a time when morality was like hill-walking in a National Park: you would cause much damage if you did not stick 'religiously' to the ancient footpaths. Not now; for after nihilism the whole nature and function of the ethical has to be conceived differently. Now, an ethic has to be a rationale for and an incitement to innovative and productive action. *Just* keeping pure and not committing any sins, *just* fulfilling your obligations, *just* being a faithful servant, *just* doing the right thing – these conceptions, once potent, are nowadays barely ethical at all. They fall too far short. They scarcely even reach the starting-gate. An ethic has to be a way of creating new values; it has got to be a way of redeeming our life by giving it aesthetic worth. Since there isn't any 'objective' or metaphysical truth or value, we ourselves have to create and to redeem our world. Ethics is now that task. It's big: we've got to do what God used to do for us.

It is in this sense that I say unkindly that there hasn't yet been any Christian ethics to speak of. In historic Christianity there was no allowance for human creative activity, human drive and ambition, or human ethical innovation. God had monopoly control of all creativity, of moral value and of historical change.

By the standard of today's needs, traditional Christian morality was a matter of doing your best to avoid attracting God's displeasure, by reducing your sins to the minimum. It was a matter of working to rule, and keeping your head down and your nose clean. It was a matter of cultivating virtues which were attitudinal rather than world-changing. Even when the ethic, at its most vigorous, recommended the cardinal virtues of prudence, justice, temperance and fortitude, you were never very clearly told exactly what addition to the world the possession of these virtues would equip you to make. It seemed that the virtues were ornamental rather than instrumental. You weren't ever quite told to *forget* your 'soul' and to get out and build something that would endure a while. The traditional theology of work was like the rationale for the labour of monks and prisoners: it was not intrinsically worthwhile, but it kept them out of mischief and gave idle hands something to do. No classical tome on Christian ethics ever suggested the truth, which is that to project and to create a life-work of some kind is the best way to gain life-satisfaction. But then, the very phrase 'Christian ethics' is itself of rather recent origin. Historically there was no such subject; there was only a penitential discipline and a moral theology. That is, Christianity didn't *have* an ethic in the sense of a theory of creative and constructive this-worldly and historical action. It had only a wretched and ugly theory of sin – what the sins were, how to diagnose them and assess their gravity, what therapies to prescribe. It wasn't about how to make something good, but only about how to make and keep yourself pure.

Traditional Christian consciousness was an internalized master-slave relationship. You had a set of standards whose true character you did not understand. You believed them to be eternal verities, and you lived subject to their extremely strict rule. You felt yourself to be under discipline. And when in due course all these standards got themselves demythologized, people naturally feared that a culture without any remaining old-style platonic or theological standards would be slovenly and anarchistic. Conservative believers and moralists feel for the modern world exactly the same contempt that soldiers feel for civilians. Lazy and comfortable; no discipline, no excellence, no strength and no real camaraderie. But this contempt for modernity is an error, like Solzhenitsyn's contempt for the West. Consider this decisive counter-example: we find that it takes just as much discipline to use language well today, when meaning is just the flux of current usage, as it took in the old days when meanings were supposedly timeless and defined by Academies. Today's sort of discipline is self-discipline, involving, among other things, minute attentiveness to detail and continual responsiveness to change. Right-wing platonism thinks the only sort of discipline there can be is its own sort: élite rule, absolute standards, strict repression. But it is wrong, for there is also the newer kind of self-discipline for creative activity, once the preserve of artists and now becoming diffused through the culture.

This discussion should have suggested along what general lines we must invent Christian ethics. A modern Christian doesn't bother about saving her soul; instead she prefers to lose it in her work. This work is the work of love. It is a creative and redemptive work by which, most typically, value is bestowed upon people who would otherwise lack it. Love saves the world and justifies the poor, the wicked and the ungodly – including even you and me. A simple way into Christian ethics is to take the whole of the traditional theology of redemption as our programme. Everything they thought God had already done for them, we are going to have to do for each other. Only, today people don't need to be saved from sin so much as from meaninglessness, worthlessness and nihilism. Christian ethics certainly seeks to change the world, but it does not begin with detailed tinkering. The *first* task is to create enough value, to inject enough meaning and weight into our human world to make life worth living at all. Brace yourself for the task of doing the work of God.

But does it make sense to propose such a task? We face a daunting contradiction: on the one hand the age seems to call for heroic ethical creationism, while yet on the other hand meaning and value have become so objective and dispersed that the creative individual is disappearing. The age won't let us do what the age seems to call for.

In all modern philosophies of language, the sign and structures, it is generally accepted that the world is just the human world, that this human world of ours is a communications network, and that it is constituted within and by language. Furthermore, the code precedes the message, and society precedes the individual.

You and I can produce our particular utterances only because we have all had the public language inscribed upon us. It is a vast system of flowing interconnected meanings in which everything just is its own relations with and differences from everything else. Furthermore, every meaning-difference is also a value-difference. We can see this most clearly in an archaic society, where it is very obvious that the lines or boundaries that define normality are both differences between meanings and also differences of value; but the same is true of more developed societies. We get access to the world of meaning only insofar as every meaning can be *felt* as a comparative value-tone in our sensibility. *Every* difference is *felt* in a way that makes meaning and value coextensive.[2] And meaning and value are also *public*.

Now, the consequence of this insight is that both meaning and value have escaped from individual control and have become dispersed throughout all the objective world. Of both alike it must then be said that *all this* is a pre-existent and public reality into which I have been inducted and in which I am maintained. It is not in my power to alter it by any private fiat of my will. Every day I take in and I emit many thousands of words. The words I take in keep my own usages very closely aligned with everybody else's. But with words I don't just take in meanings; I also take in values. Our values are also carried in the language, for they are the flavours or overtones by which we smell words. So mark this: exactly the same mechanism that keeps me semantically lined up with everyone else must also be at work to keep me evaluatively lined up with everybody else. What then is the scope for value-creation, or for a Christian ethic that stands out against the world? There is of course a sense in which Society is the Creator, because my individual performances stand in relation to the whole structure much as the individual used to stand before God. But just as God did not give the individual much opportunity to be really creative under the old dispensation, so Society doesn't seem to leave the individual much scope under the new dispensation. Society writes the tunes and I am free to play them at its bidding, and that's all.

We see here why Objective Idealism, structuralism and similar philosophies can so easily be turned in a quietistic, conservative or pessimistic direction. And we see also why in them ethics tends to become so dispersed that it is in danger of vanishing as a distinct subject. In order to bring back some creative freedom into the world post-structuralist philosophies develop theories of the disorderly anti-social sign, of meanings that won't stay still, and of transgression. But now we see that post-structuralism's relation to what went before it is surprisingly like Christianity's relation to the Jewish Law – and we begin to see the shape of a possible Christian ethics.

This book can be read on its own, but it belongs with *The Long-Legged Fly* (1987) and at a number of points rests on positions established, as I hope, in that book. Once again I have to thank Linda Woodhead for her assistance and suggestions, and Linda Allen for her typing.

D.C.

1

CHRISTIAN ETHICS AS THE CREATION OF HUMAN VALUE

The end of the old realistic conception of God as an all-powerful and objective spiritual Being independent of us and sovereign over us; more generally, the end of the old habit in all intellectual questions of referring things to a superior, unifying, ideal realm above, and with that also the end of fixed essences and unchanging objective truth – all this makes it now possible and even necessary for us to create a Christian ethic, almost as if for the first time. We are no longer like people who find ourselves in a ready-made City, surrounded by structures and values and Powers already fully operative and leaving us with little to do but purify our hearts and keep the rules. The cosmos no longer seems to us like a pre-established household in that old way. On the contrary, it seems to be we ourselves who within our cultural history have gradually evolved both our picture of the world and our values. That is, it is we ourselves who alone make truth, make value, and so have formed the reality that now encompasses us. But this in turn means that the ethical now matters to us more urgently than ever, for our choices, our valuations and the direction in which we turn our creative activity are primal, and make our world.

When just over a century ago moral thinking at last became truly critical, it therewith became clear that the philosophers hitherto had not yet thought about morality, but had merely preached it. They had accepted the notion that there was already only one truly moral morality, and they had set themselves to defend it. They had thought that there was some kind of objective and constraining moral order in the cosmos at large, rather as in the state there is an objective and constraining system of civil law. So they supposed that there was a cosmic and noumenal moral order, like a natural legal system; or more modestly, that there was at the very least a fixed human essence and a fixed nature of human happiness and well-being. In one way or another they were convinced, as so many people still wish to be convinced, that there are Invisible Guide-rails out there and already laid down. They thought – as most people thought, until the nineteenth century – that these Invisible Guide-rails were part of the unchanging order of things. They were extra-historical, platonic and timeless. And so engrained was this error that it altogether blinded people to the obvious, namely that the moral realm is continuous with and of a piece with culture generally. It is – and how could it *not* be? – human, ever-changing and full of accidents and untidinesses. But in obstinate defiance of what was before their eyes the philosophers laboured mightily to prove that morality is unchanging, rationally self-consistent and unitary. Its relation to the manifest was portrayed as the relation of the noumenal to the phenomenal, the universal to the particular, the necessary to the contingent and the ideal to the actual, for after twenty-three centuries people could still think of nothing better than this docile repetition of what Plato had told them to think. And then they tried to prove – in a non-circular way, if possible – the morality of morality, its moral title to our conformity. They understood the ethical in a completely precritical fashion, as our submission to a pre-existent One True Morality – as if the ideal were already transcendently actual, prior to us.

All of this shows that the tradition of our thinking about morality has been for all these centuries in just the same muddle as the tradition of our thinking about religion (*and* about metaphysics, *and* physics and so on). Heidegger called the way of thinking involved 'onto-theo-logy'. Discontented with the passing show of existence, we seek to go beyond it to a pre-eminent, self-present, foundational and controlling Reality. We want to regard our world as secondary, a mere shadow of something prior and greater that lies beyond it. We take the patterns in terms of which we organize our own experience and we objectify them, founding them in an order of independent timeless things on the far side of experience. There are people who project out their own fears as ghosts which then return and make them more fearful than ever, so that their problem becomes self-exacerbating – and thus it is also with us. We have been in the grip of illusions, fantasies about timeless intellectual spooks that by successfully claiming the right to control all our thought and conduct have thoroughly corrupted us. No wonder that some have felt we need a generation of nihilism to spring-clean our minds. We need, it is said, a moratorium on the use of all the words that designate moral and religious objects. We need time for all the untruths and illusions, all the false overtones, to die away before a cleaner and more wholesome moral and religious vocabulary can take shape.

Unfortunately change does not happen in that way. In practice there is always a long messy period during which the new incoming ways of thinking coexist very awkwardly with the old. During this period the new is at a disadvantage. It seems to be incomprehensibly and almost blasphemously wrong-headed. The difficulty is that the platonists remain dominant, and all their ways of thinking are still in possession of the field. We are all guided by their assumption that knowledge is knowledge of the ideal intelligible order out there, truth is correspondence with it, and virtue is conformity to it. In short, the platonists have already *defined* knowledge, truth and virtue in onto-theo-logical terms. The result is 'realism': theory in science, ethics, religion and so on is thought of as being true insofar as it 'clothes in words' or replicates in language the structure of an intelligible reality out there, be it a physical law, a divine attribute, or an eternal moral verity. The Intelligible as captured in our thought and re-presented in language is a photocopy of the pre-existent Intelligible out there. Such is 'literal truth', and the newer ways of thinking that reject this onto-theo-logy must appear to the platonist to be rejecting knowledge, truth and virtue as such. We anti-realists are believed to be saying that modern physics is not about anything, that there isn't really a God, and that there can be no absolute values. Once this interpretation of what we are saying has become established, it is not easy for us to make any further progress. Because the platonist and the modern anti-realist have quite different conceptions of knowledge, truth and virtue, they find it hard to do more than glare at each other in mutual incomprehension.

Platonism and anti-realism have no common vocabulary. But perhaps I can do something to show the disadvantages of platonism and the preferability of other ways of thinking. In particular, I want to argue that ethical platonism is unhelpful now because it answers the wrong question.

Whether they were religious or secular, moralists in pre-Nietzchean times were as we have been saying usually realists. There was an objective moral order out there, just one, and they were its salesmen, busily persuading us of the advantageousness of disciplining our practice to its requirements. When the sceptic asked, 'Why should I be moral?', it was as if he too frankly conceded that there was indeed only one morality and it was already out there. He did not disbelieve in its *existence*, but merely felt disinclined to submit to its yoke until he had been convinced that he must do so.

When the question about morality is framed in this way, then the issue becomes one of the *advantageousness* of morality. Plato's tough guy says: 'Why should I be moral? I know what I want and I know how to get it. I can look after myself. Morality? – What's in it for me?' And Plato's response is to try to prove that there is indeed something in it for the tough guy. Even by his own egoistic criteria it is to the tough guy's advantage to accept the restraints of morality; and here Plato's arguments sound like the arguments for being a tame ox rather than a wild one. How would you persuade a wild bull that he would be better off domesticated? By pointing out that the hedge that limits his freedom also keeps out his competitors, and secures for him a quiet life with a steady supply of food and females. What more can he want? It's rational for him to remain on the farm voluntarily.

However, none of this is relevant today, for the question has changed. Reflection has demythologized us to an extent that would have astonished Thrasymachus. Our problem now is an all-pervading meaninglessness and emptiness. We are too historically-minded to be interested in the idea of a timeless moral order out there, just one; and we are also aware of the extent to which everything, including our own nature and our own desires, is constituted within language and is mutable and contingent. There is no bedrock and nothing is fixed, not my identity nor my sexuality nor my categories of thought, nothing. But now as nihilism looms, and where everything is contingent and there is no Truth – how is it possible for me to perform an ethical deed? How can I *do*? How is reality-producing, value-realizing creative action possible to us? (If it isn't, we've had it; we pass away like a puff of smoke.) Thus morality as last becomes something really important. Plato had set out to answer the childish question, 'Why should I keep the rules?' and gave the even more childish answer, 'Because it's in your own interest'. But now there *are* no rules prior to us, and the ethical question is 'How can we so act as to make our own insignificant lives worthwhile?'

Can I, then, do a deed that can save me from dissolution? I cannot continue to live unless I can do something to inject some value into life. Everything, but every thing, that people formerly lived by is gone. Now I need to know how I can live, after Truth. The old myth of a saving Superknowledge waiting to be discovered, of a pre-designed state of blessedness that is somehow already prepared for us and is *there*, just waiting for us to find it and enter it, is dispelled and beyond hope of resuscitation. The human condition is utterly gratuitous and contingent, and there is nothing out there antecedently for us to live for or to live by. Our existence is *de trop* and we are thrown back upon ourselves. There is no external measure of our value or disvalue – and *therefore* our life is exactly as precious or as insignificant as we ourselves make it out to be. The value we assign to it is its only, *and so its true*, value. In which case it is rational to prefer, to choose and to affirm that ethic and view of life which maximizes the value of our life. Religion may thus nowadays be viewed as the institution that functions to maintain our will to value. Hence our modern religion of individual human rights. They are fictions, but since all is fiction and there is no Truth they are after all *not* just fictions, but great moral achievements. That ethic deserves to be honoured by us which most highly magnifies the worth of each human being. Since we know damned well that our life is *objectively* worthless, since there is no objective point of view upon us of any moral consequence to us, then it's all up to us and we are entirely free to establish, if we can, the convention that each human life is unique and of infinite worth. Established, it's true – as true as anything can be.

The morality that it is rational to prefer is the morality with the greatest power to inject value into life, and that morality is the Christian morality, which gives worth to the worthless and justifies the ungodly. To make precious something, such as me, which hitherto was mere trash – that is Gospel. But the moment in which we see the point of Christian morality – *after* the death of God, *after* the Cosmos, *after* Truth – is also the moment in which we grasp that modern morality has become self-consciously and thoroughly creationist. We begin to understand that through the differentiation of our language and our practices we create everything. There is only one moral imperative left: Create value! Value is Grace! So as I suggested earlier, the ethical question becomes: 'How then can we find the *strength* to create; how is productive, value-realizing action possible?'

With this question, the full weight of the ethical becomes apparent. It is concerned with how we are to create ourselves and our world. If I seek to put forward humanitarian Christian ethics as the best answer we can give, I must simultaneously admit that there has scarcely yet been any serious Christian ethics at all. In historic Christianity God arrogated all true creativity to himself, and human creativity was denied, not affirmed. If ethics is concerned with keeping pre-established rules and not falling out of favour, then yes, there has been Christian ethics; but if ethics is concerned with the absolute creation of value, then there has not yet been Christian ethics, or at least not officially; for officially only God made things and set standards. Nevertheless, and in spite of the record hitherto, I shall argue that a new Christian ethics can be invented which is a relevant answer to the modern ethical question. This proposal may help to resolve a paradox, for why is it that around the world vast numbers of people express great admiration for Christian ethics when (intellectually speaking) the topic is as good as non-existent? Their real religion is the modern Western religion of humanitarianism, liberal democracy and the struggle to establish ever more human rights, and they are in effect saying that they want to think of this modern secular faith and ethic as being in spirit Christian. But this hunch or desire of theirs doesn't yet have a theoretical justification. For example, historically the language of faith was always monarchical in tendency rather than democratic. Furthermore, the New Testament teaches us not to claim but to waive our rights, and some of the greatest theologies are ferocious onslaughts on the notion that we human beings can have any rights or merits at all. The fact is that before the nineteenth century Christianity was scarcely at all liberal, humanitarian, democratic or concerned about people's rights. Yet people persistently believe that these things are

'Western values' and are Christian, so we must invent a Christianity that will justify their faith. Let's make them right; let's make their error into truth.

If we can do this, it will be *only* because the old almighty God has gone and Christian ethics can at last come of age. While the old God was about, he prevented Christian ethics from becoming truly creative. He alone made history, had all the power and fixed all the values. He alone was in the strongest sense an *agent*, a doer. Christian ethics could not become *Christian* while he was about, because it is Christian only insofar as it has the pure creative power to change the rules and to confer value on what would otherwise remain worthless. Only through the death of that God does Christian ethics at last acquire the duty and the authority to create value *ex nihilo*, which marks it as truly Christian and enables it to redeem our life.

Let me be boringly but necessarily repetitious: an ethic adequate to modern needs has to show how a human being can be a real creator with entrepreneurial drive and flair, someone with the self-confidence and the capacity to conceive and to execute an original work, autonomously – and someone who has the force of character to be able if necessary to conscript others to help complete the work. An ethic in the sense here under discussion is a text that stimulates the reader to think that she or he can really make something good. All flesh is as grass and our subjective life is transient. My much-vaunted 'self' is little more than an epiphenomenon of language. Soon I'll be gone and so will you, but in the meantime we can rejoice in life together if we find reason to believe that we can together make something with our names on it, something we thought up and we got done, something into which *we* put the value, something we worked on and we worked for. To work together and to make something is life-satisfaction.

... but you'd never have guessed it from the Christian tradition, which did not celebrate drive, creativity or job-satisfaction. Or rather, it did – but only in God. Only God created all being and value, controlled the future and fixed truth. Human imagination, force of character and self-expression in creative work began to be officially celebrated and religiously-permissible only with the dawn of Romanticism. There had been plenty of figures in the older tradition who had *possessed* such qualities, but the religious ideology to which they were committed prevented the recognition of these qualities as being Christian. Officially, the creative imagination was Satan-inspired fantasy and creative action was Luciferean presumption. God had so far done everything for us as to leave us with little to do except thank him and try to refrain from offending him by disturbing anything. Of course we were such hopeless creatures that however carefully we tiptoed about we still couldn't help but offend him, but God had mercifully provided lots of good works for us to do to sweeten his temper. Augustine lists some fourteen or so of these works of mercy (*Enchiridion*, 72), but makes it only too plain that a Christian does not help the poor from humanitarian motives, nor with any plan of abolishing poverty. The external or objective effect of a deed is of no consequence. Only your own inner purity matters, and in case you forget it you should learn to practise an absurdity that Augustine calls 'spiritual almsgiving', and give to yourself.¹ The poverty of the poor as such is of no interest to Augustine. A Christian should think only of himself, of his sins, and of how he can become pleasing to God. Thus if I give money to a poor man, my action is meritorious insofar as I do it only for the sake of my own relation to God, and not for the poor man's sake. This remained the motive for Christian philanthropic action during its classic period, the fifteenth to seventeenth centuries. Those who founded schools, almshouses and hospitals did so, not principally in order to change things for others in this world, but in obedience to Christ and in order to improve their own chances of salvation in the next world. So much for Christian ethics.

And a strange paradox runs through much of the tradition. Its leading figures were robust and forceful characters: why then do they urge us to become morally impotent and timid as rabbits? The New Testament epistles seem often to be recommending to us the character of an idealized Victorian maiden with a crushed ego, passive, sweet-natured, docile, unfailingly inoffensive, loving and meek, waiting uncomplainingly for Mr Right to come along and finally relieve her of the last vestiges of personal responsibility for her own fate. *That* is what we should be like — or so we are told.

Yet Paul himself was not at all like this. His text, bursting with perhaps-unconscious self-revelation, shows him to be much better than his teaching, a fine man, a difficult character, domineering, insecure, workaholic, rampant, driving and objectionable, a man capable of great religious exaltation, of writing a text and of building a human community. He was clearly a real human being, a high-class figure worthy of the most cordial detestation and respect, a splendid and memorable old monster. We are speaking of a very familiar conflict within Paul's text. Ostensibly, he praises an insipid and mouselike character, forgiving, tender-hearted and ineffectual. He has to praise such a character-type because his theology demands it. If my self-valuation is very low and I am desperate to avoid offending someone who has limitless power over me, then of course I must become a feminine masochist. But while Paul praises one character-type, he actually *exhibits* another which is altogether more trenchant, vigorous and deplorable. That very ill-repressed side of Paul (like Tolstoy?) stands for the real Christian ethic. It will have to wait a long time before it can come fully into the open and express itself in words. Meanwhile for centuries writers will go on commending the traditional Down's-syndrome Christian personality-type, loving, guileless and wouldn't-hurt-a-fly, a person who has made himself so utterly neutered and harmless that not even God himself can discover any grounds for getting annoyed with him. And yet in century after century the real characters of the great figures were joyfully at odds with their professed ideals.

So, strangely, there have from the first been two levels in the Western Christian tradition. At the manifest and dominant level the faith appeared to teach an absolutist view of God and a masochistic doctrine of redemption. The way to release was through utter passivity: God must have his way with us and do everything to us, in us, for us. He must act first, without bothering to wait for our invitation or even co-operation. He must glory in the triumph of his will in us and upon us, and we must will only his glorying over us.

But there was also a latent and repressed level at which Christianity was and knew itself to be a movement of human emancipation. From the first it was producing strikingly forceful, dramatic and creative characters. And one might say that in these characters, and at this largely unconscious level, the possibility of an authentic Christian ethic was being maintained, explored and transmitted to us. An unconscious tradition has reached us as well as the conscious one, and it is the more interesting of the two.

2

THE END OF TWO-WORLDS DUALISM

The task of Christian ethics, so I am arguing, coincides with the task of the traditional theology of redemption. A text about Christian ethics will first and foremost set out to show how by what we do we can redeem our transient life from meaninglessness or worthlessness. We may not amount to much in ourselves, but we are capable of productive value-realizing work, and we can give each other value just by valuing one another. It is rational to adopt that morality which sets the highest value on human life, namely a liberal Christian humanitarianism which continually invents and then struggles for the effective social entrenchment of fresh human rights. These rights are fictions that it is good for us to affirm and to make into social facts. Furthermore, it is also rational to follow those social practices and rituals that help to give us courage and to strengthen us in our affirmation of the value of our life and in our ethical productivity, or power of moral innovation. For this reason it is good to attend Holy Communion frequently, even though we certainly do not hold the supernatural beliefs traditionally associated with the rite. A modern Christian still finds in the service an efficacious symbol of the faith, that is of the redemptive and new-world-making power of love and companionship (literally, 'bread-togetherness').

When Christian faith has become fully modern and humanistic, it says that *we* must create value, *we* must save each other, *we* must redeem our life, *we* are the new regenerate humanity. Christian action creates and saves the world. Its potency in these respects is superior to that of straight secular humanism, whether liberal or marxist, because Christian humanism is religious and explicitly presents itself as a temporalization and humanization of God. Thus the human being acquires a dignity and a status that is directly derived from the ancient holiness and worshipfulness of God. God indeed just was a symbol of the goal towards which our moral development is heading and of the dignity to which we should ultimately attain. Christian humanism does not wholly dispense with God but retains precisely the God *who dispenses himself to us*, dying into us and communicating to us his own attributes.

The New Testament and the Creed describe Christ as God's *only* Son and say that there is no way to God except through Christ. This means that God is wholly incarnated in Christ and in those who are Christ's, that is, the human race. God has died into Christ and there is no longer any extra-human God. To believe in any objective and extra-human God is to be in darkness and not yet to have understood the completeness of God's hominization:

> God Appears and God is Light
> To those poor souls who dwell in Night,
> But does a Human Form Display
> To those who Dwell in Realms of Day . . .
>
> Thou art a Man, God is no more;
> Thine own humanity learn to adore,
> For that is my Spirit of Life.
> Awake, arise to Spiritual Strife . . .[1]

Now if God has thoroughly and completely temporalized himself and dispersed himself into humanity, there can no longer be any reason to disparage time, action and the body. In the Christian myth these things have all now been given divine dignity. Unfortunately, in classical Christianity (so-called) the human world was devalorized and the value expropriated from it was projected up into the timeless world above. The consequences of this for Christian ethics need now to be considered.

Historically, Christian ethics never set out to be a complete ethic for this world and this present life. In the New Testament it was an *interimsethik* before the *Parousia*, that is, it was designed to serve only for the short interim-time that remained before history ended with the coming of God in Judgment. And in fact the belief that the days were numbered and that only a few generations or at most a few centuries were left before the End of all things lingered on, fading only slowly, until the Enlighten-ment. But it became overlaid by the more salient picture of Christian ethics as an *interimsethik* before life in the heavenly world above. The most thoroughgoing version of this view was monasticism, according to which the best Christian was the person who had fled from time, action, history and human love, who had in fact repudiated all normal human responsibilities, in order to spend the whole remainder of his life waiting in the vestibule of Heaven. This outlook was not a temporary aberra-tion. It became dominant quite early in the Patristic period and has never been decisively repudiated by either the Greek or the Latin churches. Yet where it is present there can be no Christian ethic, but only despair and defeatism. To say that the best Christian is the person who has opted out of normal human political, economic and sexual activity (and conflict) is to give up. The monastery was a hospice for those who were terminally sick of life, and a standing denial of the Christian Gospel.

Yet we must stay with it, because its psychology is our psychology. The monastery is the main reason why there is still almost no Christian ethic. Even in ruins, its ideology remains potent.

The monk's path to salvation was determined by what Heidegger and Derrida have taught us to call the metaphysics of presence. This metaphysics is dissatisfied by the secondary, mediated and never-complete character of our life. It is on the lookout for something independent and sheerly given, something that just is itself, unmistakably. In particular it yearns for that which would constitute the highest fulfilment of its hopes, namely the immediate absolute knowledge of absolute Being, in a state of timelessness. Absolute Being is Being that has completely got itself together. It is *totum simul, actus purus*, everything all at once, all there, infallibly and completely self-subsistent and present to itself. To be all this it clearly has to be timeless, and so does absolute knowledge, which is envisaged as like being able to see every aspect of a thing all at once and unmistakably, so that one is quite clear that one sees all that it is and exactly why in every respect it has to be just what it is. At the summit of the monk's value-scale therefore was the Vision of God, which was pure timeless intellectual contemplation of the eternal necessity of the infinite perfection of the divine essence. The more one

reflects on this stupendous ambition, the more one sees that it is
derived from the early infant's desire for absolute possession of
the Beloved Object. Compared with such an aim, real life –
mediated, transient and incomplete – is a shadow-play.

In terms of the traditional contrast between Jew and Greek (a
contrast which, it must be admitted, Derrida has sought to
undermine[2]) the monk was wholly on the Greek side. On his
value-scale the highest ranking was given to knowledge, to the
sense of sight, to the indicative, and to the contemplative life.
Beatitude is to perceive with perfect clarity that what is so,
eternally must be so. By contrast, the Jew – and I repeat that I am
invoking a traditional stereotype – the Jew gave preference to
righteousness, to the sense of hearing, to the imperative and to the
active life. Beatitude was then perfectly to hear and to obey God's
will in one's social relationships.

Now it would not be quite correct to say that classical
Christianity ranked knowledge higher than virtue. To cite just
one example, in Christian angelology the seraphim (who are
perfect in love) rank higher than the cherubim (who are perfect in
knowledge). But the love here in question is a God-directed
contemplative disposition of the soul. It is oriented towards 'the
spiritual marriage' and is not active or social, so that one may still
accurately say that the whole monkish tradition, established in
early times and still not fully overcome, invariably ranked
contemplation higher than agapeistic neighbourly action. The
highest sort of love was the *inactive*, theoretical love which was
called 'the love of God'.

There is more, and worse, to come. Even before the rise of
monasticism to supreme prestige in the church, the linkage
between holiness and virginity had become established. The holy
was that which was segregated, unspotted, intact, unused and
innocent. Already the suggestion is that activity as such is
contaminating, for it takes a thing away from the pristine and
perfect condition in which it left the Creator's hand. That which
is used becomes spotted, and sexual defilement is dreaded above
all else. In Christian art the nude, and more especially the female
nude, comes to be associated with temptation, sin, guilt, corruption and death. There is an astonishingly strong cultural dread
and denial of female sexuality and of the imagination, which is
seen as Satan-promoted.

The upshot of all this is that the dominant morality in classical Christianity took the form of avoidance-behaviour. The aim was not to achieve anything, but so far as possible to commit no sins. The most highly regularized avoidance-behaviour just *was* 'the religious life'. It was the Honours course for those who sought salvation. Christianity survived only because the church retained the possibility of a pass degree, since a lay person, living a neighbour-oriented life in the world and obeying only the *mandata*, might still just make it to Heaven. Even so orthodox a writer as K. E. Kirk says that the doctrine of the *mandata* 'saved Christianity', and emphasizes the strangeness of the fact that no early Christian writer can be found who asserts that monastic asceticism is untrue to Christianity.[3]

This last point reminds us that the ethical significance of religious doctrines is amazingly differently perceived in different periods. In the modern period, since around 1800, we have become more and more accustomed to think that the doctrine of the Incarnation asserts the embodiment of the Holy within, and therefore the sacralization of, everything that is material, mundane and human. The Incarnation is now perceived as blurring the distinctions between God and man, sacred and secular etc., so that loving God and loving your needy neighbour become more and more closely assimilated to each other. Yet in the past people evidently did not see the ethical meaning of the Incarnation in this way at all, or the enclosed contemplative could never have been regarded as the highest Christian type.

However that may be, the legacy of our terrible past is that the Christian (and especially the European Christian) is still afflicted by paralysing anxiety about time and action. By their very nature they appear to threaten her or him with loss of presence, a leakage away of personal integrity and the forfeiture of salvation. Two illustrations may help to show the extreme severity of Christian anxiety. The first is simply the nightmarish popular theology of purgatory, with all that it has to say about guilt, punishment and time. But secondly, and even more revealing, the sixteenth-century Christian had become so morally impotent that redemption had perforce to take the form of theological rape. I am not blaming Calvin himself for the coarse sexual violence of his language – total depravity, the bondage of the will, unconditional election, irresistible grace – but I am saying that where people have been made to have a strong sense of sin their sense of self-worth is so reduced that they can obtain ecstatic release only by suffering violation. Their theology of conversion and their religious experience therefore become modelled on rape-fantasies. In the literature of the sixteenth and seventeenth centuries we repeatedly encounter the notion that the soul needs to be ravished and just loves to be ravished,[4] an idea that our culture could well have done without.

Our task, then, is to redeem people from the old masochistic 'orthodox' Christianity by curing them of the sense of sin, restoring their self-esteem and vindicating Christian action. It needs to be shown not just that we can act without the disabling fear of losing our salvation, but that we can go further and act creatively, giving value to our life and to each other and so saving ourselves.

A number of solutions have already been attempted. The early Protestant solution is roughly what Max Weber described as intramundane asceticism. Outwardly secular, I choose to retain a thoroughly monkish psychology and seek to avoid corruption by the world in which I live. I am a monk in plain clothes, outwardly one thing but inwardly another like a spy, a person with a dual identity.

Only we must go further than Weber in our interpretation. Having suffered his theological rape the early Protestant rejoiced to find himself a hollow channel, an empty shell, a drained husk. He was now relieved of responsibility and could see himself as a tool or medium through which God acted. God had always been thought of as the Lord of history, the only historical agent. Our human attempts to act rarely turn out as we mean them and are all too often self-subverting. God alone is *strong* enough to act effectively; and in addition, because he is eternal he can bring about effects in time without suffering a debilitating loss of self-presence as he acts. So the early Protestant, trying for the first time to conceive how an ethically productive secular Christian life might be possible, had to view himself as a vehicle for God's action, a tool in God's hand. Good works can get themselves done only insofar as God does them through me, so that they are not really my works but his. I lie back and let God get on with it. God can do for me what I can't do for myself, namely, *act*.

Such a theology, with its uncomfortable linguistic contortions, could not last for long. Something better took shape among the early Romantics. The self is a process of becoming, and it develops through its own self-expression in action. So the old two-worlds dualism was thrown forward and enhistorized. The contrast between the actual and the ideal now became a contrast between the present age and the future New Jerusalem to be built on earth by human labour. The perfect world had in the past been understood in entirely supernatural terms, and it would have been absurd to suggest that human beings could play any part in bringing it into existence. The faithful were instructed simply to watch and pray, and to wait in patient hope. Now, however, the Kingdom of God was increasingly equated with a fully Christ-ianized state of human society. Every Christian ought to be playing some small part in building it, whether by campaigning for social reform or more simply by working quietly for the diffusion of the Christian spirit and values through social life.

Although this programme was a vast improvement upon every previous conception of the task of Christian ethics, it was still flawed. It distinguished between the actual and the ideal, very sharply. But I am a product of this present, imperfect, actual world, and in order to engage with it I am compelled myself to accept and act within the terms in which it operates and understands itself. So I must surely suffer the same fate as other idealistic revolutionaries: the temporizing, the ugly necessities of the revolutionary struggle must corrupt me and prevent me from realizing the revolutionary goal. The only way I can avoid this pessimistic conclusion is by falling back upon the older theologies. I start fancying that a spirit better and stronger than me has taken control of my life, so that even if I do make a cock-up he will over-rule me and ensure that everything comes out all right just the same. Thus I find I have to renounce my personal responsibility for the way things go almost as soon as I assumed it – and Christian ethics goes into retreat again. And on the larger scale, the great legitimating narratives about progress and Providence which in the nineteenth century sustained socialists, liberals and many Christians have now broken down. It now cannot be said too emphatically that nothing is guaranteed and nothing says that things *have* to go one way rather than another. The old objectified theological drama of creation, judgment and redemption is now hominized. It has become the drama of our own responsibility for creating our own future. Our life and our death are in our own hands. We have appropriated and enhistorized apocalyptic. In this new order of things, in which there is no supernatural order, no life after death and no promise of help – except insofar as all these things are now in human heads and hands – in this new order we must learn to use religion in a rather novel and conscious way as a tool of self-training, self-schooling.

One lesson we have to school ourselves to learn, after the end of traditional liberal Christianity and socialism, is that there will be no final success. No End of all things, no communist society, no New Jerusalem, no Sabbath Rest of the Saints, no final victory. Rather, we'll just soldier on indefinitely.

This idea is not wholly novel. Biologically-minded philosophers such as Hobbes and Leibniz, who recognized that our life is an endless striving activity or endeavour, pointed out long ago the difficulty of postulating an End-state in which striving has ceased while yet life continues. Kant was so much under the influence of the metaphysics of presence that he remained convinced that the highest good must be attainable, even though he clearly saw that it could not be realized within the present historical order. For similar reasons a strong theological tradition also insisted that the final perfection of the self cannot be achieved in time. One is forbidden to claim perfection. The most that a catholic saint or a Spirit-born protestant may claim is a brief foretaste of beatitude. The self, or the historical process, may approach asymptotically towards perfection, may enjoy a brief foretaste of perfection, and may cherish vivid images of perfection. But the real thing has got to stay just out of reach; in Kantian terms, it is a regulative ideal.

A Christian ethics along these lines was taught half a century ago by Reinhold Niebuhr. The Marxist equivalent would be Mao-Tse-Tung's doctrine of perpetual revolution, or Foucauldian 'infinite protest'.

The standard objection is this: What's the *point* of a philosophical or religious message if it cannot promise us that we will get somewhere? People sometimes say, 'Life after death is the poor man's theodicy. If you don't believe in any life after death in which people will be compensated for all that they have suffered, what have you to say to the modern millions who face only oppression, disease and starvation?' So we reply, 'It's wrong to promise people pie in the sky when they die. An activist Christian humanism tries to get something done *now*, by education, by political and economic changes and so on.' Then they ask, 'But will the struggle go on *for ever*? Will there always be poverty and exploitation like this?' And we answer, 'Yes. You see, there was a time when people felt so awful about having lost their pie in the sky that they had to be promised pie in the future instead. But now we must do without that pie in the future. No reward is needed in order to justify the struggle. Just fight till you drop.'

Thus the guiding star, the vision of regained earthly paradise, the impossible ideal – stays out of reach. We keep striving after it, although we admit now that we will never actually grasp it. And this view of things has some merits. In particular, it leaves the ontology of the moral ideal relatively unconfused. For I admit now that the moral ideal *is* just an ideal, a dream, and will stay an ideal. This avoids the awkward paradoxes that accompany the claim that the moral life is a struggle to actualize the ideal: 'Is it then somehow real already, and with a right to be actualized; and after we've actualized it, will it still be an ideal?' – and so forth.

Yet another difficulty arises instead. We have made all too neat a disjunction between the murky struggle here below and the untarnished ideal up above. We have become super-platonic and have entrenched the is-ought distinction in a way that has seemingly made impossible any salvation at all. But this is intolerable. Salvation is full personal integration. If Christian ethics is a way to blessedness, it must aim to reconcile or to mediate the disjunctions between feeling and reason, body and mind, is and ought and so on. We must surely not so entrench the distinction that we cannot conceive its mediation.

So we move on yet again. Fully to emancipate the human agent we must overcome the duality of is and ought and find a way of saying a fully-achieved religious Yes to life. There is only one way: the way of art. Without needing to believe in progress, without needing any external certificate of the worthwhileness of what she is doing, the artist in working enjoys the best synthesis of the opposites, and therefore the nearest thing to a state of beatitude that a human being can know. Sensuous activity and spiritual ideal, means and end, body and soul, hand and heart, are one in the working. Absorbed in work, the artist becomes unselfed and experiences timelessness in time. The aim of Christian ethics is to show how the ordinary everyday living of life can become like that.

We do not yet have a Christian ethic, and the full moral emancipation of human action remains some way off. To achieve it we will need to get rid of the 'sin' and 'guilt' that still blight many people's lives. We will need to escape from the influence of two-worlds dualism and the metaphysics of presence. Especially will we need to forget the platonic idea that there's an order of higher truths out there that we have got to grasp theoretically before we can act aright. That claim reduces the moral life to the level of something like being a good soldier: you learn the ropes, you learn what is required of you and then you do it. So long as we remain in the grip of the primitive notion that the human being is in the world as a servant is in a household, no truly human morality can be framed. Our life becomes merely a routine job with a tatty list of ready-made rules. No! *We* make the truth, *we* create reality, the knowing and the doing are one. Christian ethics is an ethics *produced* by Christians.

Finally, with the rejection of the metaphysics of presence we also reject the old egoistic ethic of 'saving your soul'. I have no soul and you have no soul. A Christian is supposed to lose his life, not to save it. We die in the work. *I* died to make these sentences, and I'm gone, leaving only these marks. Because of the long influence of popular fantasies about life after death, we haven't yet developed a Christian ethics of the self. This is it: like Christ, die into your work. Accept self-scattering and self-loss. Goodbye, all, goodnight.

3

ETHICS AND THE END OF PHILOSOPHY

There was something not quite right about the way ethics was set up as a subject at the very beginning of Western thought. As a result we still to this day start our thinking about the topic in the wrong place. I shall suggest that there are two main themes. The first is that the ethical was not sufficiently criticized and was left in a condition like that of religion, unmodernized and with too many archaic elements. The second is that philosophy defined itself in terms of the primacy of theoretical knowledge, in a way that was bound eventually to leave ethics looking secondary and to give rise to all the misfortunes of the fact-value, is-ought, actual-ideal distinctions. Ethics got off to a bad start.

It should never have happened. After all, ancient philosophy had had the very best of intentions. Three great provinces were marked out, Logic, Physics and Ethics, and it was supposed to be ethics that would come out on top in the end. After Socrates at least, philosophy was supposed to be undertaken for the sake of ethics. For a very long period it was customary to present your philosophy as a prescription for the cure of human ills and an itinerary to blessedness. Popularly, philosophy was a pathway of practical wisdom at whose end stood the *summum bonum*, the goal of life.

Yet in spite of this, somehow at the very beginning of Western thought the ethical was slightly misallocated. It became a little dissociated from metaphysics, with an air of having been overlooked, as if it had come along late and were trying to squeeze itself in as best it could. Whereas physics was at a very early date rather thoroughly demythologized, making a conscious break with the queer jumbled old sacred cosmologies, ethics stayed closer to the archaic. The ethical seemed still to be from on high, with overtones of supernaturalism, religious law, transcendent authority and psychological constraint. Doubtless one factor has been that ethics is a somewhat fraught and even dangerous topic, linked as it is with the question of the legitimacy of political, religious and social authority and with people's deepest fears of social breakdown. The philosophers have often been under pressure to act as defenders of the social order, and this has made it dangerous for them thoroughly to criticize and to relocate the ethical. To this day, then, morality remains alongside religion as the chief remaining stronghold of primitive ways of thinking. When we attempt to bring it into the light and to criticize certain moral values and assumptions, certain methods of moral training and elements of moral psychology, we quickly come up against the jealously-guarded, the forbidden, the taboo, in a way (and with a ferocity) that shows us only too clearly how close the religion-morality connection remains yet. Both remain so obdurate in resisting modernization that one might be forgiven for avoiding them altogether. Consider, for example, the rather elaborately-paraded caution and even distaste with which Descartes sets these matters aside.[1] After twenty-odd centuries it was still not socially permissible to get too close to questions of morality, political authority and revealed religion. Cartesian clarity might conquer elsewhere, but in *these* areas it was still unsafe for us to do anything but remain in darkness. Remember the martyrdom of Socrates.

An unhappy situation: how did it ever develop? Since there is no philosophy but the Greek sort of philosophy,* and the way Greece set the subject up just *is* philosophy, there is a question as to how we can expect to find a standpoint from which we can see, *philosophically*, how philosophy by its very nature must slightly misallocate the ethical. But was it not in part because the very first move, the one that inaugurated philosophy, that is, the move by which Western reason came into being, actually bracketted out or at least distanced itself from the ethical, ostensibly with a view to doing it more justice at a later stage? Philosophy's idea was *first* to

---

*We recognize Indian and Chinese philosophy as being such insofar as they are like the Greek. Our concept of philosophy comes from nowhere other than Greece.

set all practical questions aside and to attempt a theoretical determination of the nature of the Cosmos and the truth of the human condition. *First*, we must gain a perspectiveless – and value-neutral? – vision of the world and of our own nature as they objectively are; *first*, too, we need a perspectiveless theoretical grasp even of moral essences themselves – and then when we have achieved this it will become clear to us, at the *second* stage, how we should live.

Two or three basic and closely-related metaphors guided philosophy in its search for a vantage-point for objective knowledge. All the metaphors in this region are optical, so let us take one from film. The GV is more objective than the CU. The CU shot, where the subject is at half-length or less, is challenging, emotive, perspectival and very 'hot'. Just the choice of camera-angle manipulates the viewer's feelings. Indeed, in CU questions of angle and slant are at the forefront. By contrast, the MS and the LS, the mid-shot and the long-shot, are many degrees cooler, and the GV, the general view, is completely cool. It is used as an establishing shot, because it is synoptic, objective and gives information quickly and economically. The angle from which a GV is shot is not emotionally important. All we require is that it give the viewer a kind of location-framework into which to fit the subsequent shots. Thus a GV of the Eiffel Tower is a visual cue that prompts us to fit what follows into our mental map of the Paris streets. Analogously we may say that philosophy sought a GV that would help us to situate, and to make sense of, the subsequent action-sequences of life.

The second metaphor is the familiar one of transcendence. I climb a tall building in order to look vertically down upon the crowded street scene below. I climb the tallest tree in order to look out across the canopy and see which way I must walk to escape from the forest. In such cases the presumption is that from the high vantage-point we can see more clearly what is going on, where we are and which way we should go. But the transcendence here invoked is subjective as well as objective. It is not only a question of seeking a panoramic overview of all that is about me, but also a matter of rising above the normal limitations of my own sense organs, ways of thinking, partialities and prejudices. Self- transcendence has to be sought, and we are bound to wonder how it can be possible. How can I outsoar my own faculties, my own interests and my own perspective upon the world – and yet remain myself?

More searchingly, what is gained *ethically* by the move to the high theoretical vantage-point? Crudely and metaphorically, the claim was that when we see where we really are we'll know which way to go. Well and good: but the move to a transcendent vantage-point has wide-ranging consequences. As our earlier metaphors suggested, the longer the shot the cooler it is and the more it slows down movement. GVs are in effect stills. So the philosopher's standpoint is timeless, passionless, cool, objective and disengaged. He will tend to portray the ethical accordingly, as general, rational and unchanging. But our actual engagement with life, in CU, is the opposite of all this: it is passionate, partial and in rapid flux. In our face-to-face ethical relations with other people there just *aren't* any unambiguously-lucid and unchanging meanings and rules. Morality is, I fear, a devious business. Consider for example the kaleidoscopically-ambiguous issue of what it is to be truthful in a sexual relationship. We cannot seriously suppose that in such a matter our difficulties would be resolved for us by a GV of timeless values. Rather we are talking of a learned social skill, rather like skill in the spoken language. Indeed, there's obviously a big overlap between the two cases, managing one's personal relationships successfully being so largely a communicational skill. But to be successful I have also got to be sensitive to the fine and rapidly shifting detail of any such relationship. I've got to be in touch with my own feelings, and to be aware of the other's. Yet if this is so how can I possibly get a better moral perspective on the relationship by abstracting away from time, contingency and the emotions, and moving to a transcendent standpoint?

However, philosophy insisted on making that move. The disinterested observation that it makes possible is the defining characteristic of Western culture. So Socrates turns his great patient unblinking Cyclopean eye upon the human scene. The big Eye takes in all the phenomena that pass before it – and philosophical thought proper begins with a strange little jump in inner space, a transcendental jump. The Eye distinguishes between the particular and fleeting phenomenon that is presented to it, and the more durable and non-phenomenal frame of understanding through which it takes in the phenomenon.

That distinction is philosophy. It is many-facetted. It is the distinction between matter and form, between a particular sequence of data and the general rule exemplified in it, between empirical instance and universal concept, between the actual and the ideal, and so on. Generally, it is the distinction between the letter posted and the slot into which it is posted; between the thing presented and the intelligible form in which it is presented, or the category to which it is assigned. The point is that just to make this distinction is to open up the intelligible world. Theory, science and Greek-type understanding have become possible.

The Eye can close now. The phenomenal realm as such is of decidedly limited interest. It has done its job by serving as a stepping-stone for the discovery of the frame, the world of ideas, the world of theory which is the philosopher's true home. The Eye is now an inward and metaphorical eye – which means that it has become more of an eye than ever. In the intellectual world visual metaphors run riot: reflection, illumination, theory, viewpoint, vision, contemplation, intuition, insight, idea, image, appearance, species, speculation and so on. The affinity between the mind and the eye, and indeed between the I and the eye, suggests a disembodied, passive and timeless picture of the philosophical mind at work: it hangs about like a video-camera in a sculpture gallery, registering the unchanging forms of intelligibles that subsist independently of it. So the philosopher saw himself as the disembodied spectator of unchanging noumenal objects.

It was a ludicrously mistaken account of the situation. Plato was of course aware that philosophy is transacted in language, but he altogether failed to grasp the extent to which the meanings of words are *not* unchanging, but are a function of the ever-changing detail of shifting human communal feeling and power-relations. The meaning of a word is just like the price of some stock or commodity on an exchange. No word has an absolute meaning and no stock has an absolute price. A stock's present value depends upon its current relations with other stocks, how people feel about it and what they are trading it at. In exactly the same way a word's meaning depends upon its relations with other words, how people feel about it and what sort of trading they are doing with it. Thus there are no fixed meanings and there are no timeless truths. A word's meaning today depends upon the state of play today and what people are doing with it today. Philosophy's visual metaphoric and its picture of itself as having moved to a higher, transcendent viewpoint led it to believe that the intelligible world is objective and unchanging. It is not: meaning is just usage, and is shifting all the time.

However, in traditional philosophy everything was supposed to have a timeless essence, an archetype in the world of forms. So among the objects that philosophical thought finds and contemplates are moral essences. And to have *thus* come upon morality, from this angle and in this way, is fateful. Morality too is going to be understood as something *first* to be understood theoretically. There are various moral essences here and they can be seen more clearly, it is held, if we abstract away from the actual living of the moral life. So the moral becomes one more timeless rational object to be understood in the light of all philosophy's founding distinctions, and in each of the following cases the essence of the moral is understood through the *second* branch of the distinction: is and ought, fact and value, actual and ideal, sense and reason, matter and form, instance and rule, appearance and reality, the changing and the unchanging, the particular and the universal. Given all this, how can we escape the most consistent, the most luminously philosophical, the most hopelessly implausible and the most mythological of moral philosophies, namely Kant's?

Worse, philosophy's distinctions – above all, the is-ought distinction – have always made the *ontology* of the ethical mystifying. The is-ought distinction implies a contrast between a world that *is* but is less than satisfactory, and a world of ideal value, a world which ought to be but unfortunately is not yet. So the moral life seems to be a struggle to actualize a potency, to convert a possibility into a fact. But as we said earlier, it is a puzzle to understand how something that does not even exist can merit being brought into being, or can be thought of as having a right to exist, or can constrain us to labour to bring it into being. And suppose we succeed, and realize it: has it in ceasing to be just ideal now *lost* its value? In any case, philosophy was also committed by its founding distinctions to supposing that because the ideas or Forms are unchanging intelligible objects they are *already*, eternally and in their own right, fully self-subsistent and more real than any phenomena. Moral essences in particular are as such more permanent and precious and in every way higher than anything merely empirical. They are fine as they are, they are as real as can be already and they have nothing at all to gain by being actualized in the phenomenal world. Indeed, Plato is most insistent that Forms cannot be adequately incarnated in phenomena, and certainly don't need to be – so that the whole way of thinking about morality which sees it as an attempt to incarnate eternal values in phenomenal deeds, lives and institutions is thus called into question. Values are eternal realities, unaffected by whether our deeds mimic them or mock them. So what have they to do with us or we with them?

Yet is should not be thought that Plato's doctrine of eternal ideal values is somehow too dated or too implausible for anyone to take it seriously any more. On the contrary, it remains almost a matter of life and death to us. If you doubt this, just try to carry through consistently the thought that your own moral disapprobation of Nazism is merely a transient and contingent natural phenomenon. Just *think* that all the values you care most deeply about are products of time and chance which will in due course be swept away by the same agencies that brought them into being. Not easy. We may smile at the innocence of those who believe in absolute moral standards, as if it made sense to suppose that our values could be abstracted away from their concrete setting in our historical life, but at the bottom of our hearts we ourselves remain platonists, for we find it very hard to imagine doing without the idea that our values have somehow got to be upheld from outside the historical order. Yet what *could* this metaphorical 'upholding' consist in?

Here we return to our ontological confusion about the status of moral objects, a muddle seemingly bequeathed to us by the very way philosophy was set up. Our values seem to be both less real and more real than things in the world of fact. Sometimes they seem to be mere potencies, shadowy not-yet-realized possibilities pleading with us, or twisting our arms to actualize them. But at other times they are pictured as super-real, enduring and independent of human vagaries. Yet if they are *not* already real, how can we think of them as getting any leverage on us; and if on the contrary they *are* real independently of us, then they must be self-sufficient and the picture of them as needing to be realized, and as exerting pressure upon us, becomes absurd.

It begins to look as if the whole notion of moral objects as being out there with some degree of reality or other, whether less or more, is a mystification. Why do people feel they must objectify their moral and religious beliefs? Because they think these beliefs matter a very great deal. Cultural beliefs are projected on to the cosmos in the hope of entrenching them. If I really think of my beliefs as *just* recent cultural fictions I seem to find it hard to muster anything more than an ironical allegiance to them. But that is intolerable. In matters of morality and religion our allegiance has to be wholehearted. So I express my sense that moral allegiance has got to be unconditional by objectifying my values as cosmic unalterable facts. Now, I say, they are *not* just optional; they are compulsory and they cannot be budged.

To this day we can find ourselves sympathizing with these feelings. For example, only two or three centuries ago the most lurid and drawn-out spectacles of torture that the human mind could devise were still being mounted in public in European cities with the church's full collaboration, so as to edify the populace.[2] Everyone who reads these pages is likely to be strongly committed to humanitarian values, and to the conviction that Christian values and humanitarian values coincide; but it is very disturbing to us to realize how very recently these cherished values of ours came into being and how very uncertain is their standing in public opinion. Humanitarians were, from 1819, people who believed that Jesus was merely human and, from the 1830s, people who followed Comte's religion of humanity. From the 1850s a humanitarian was a philanthropist, a person of humane principles, but such principles were widely ridiculed as wet and wimpish throughout the nineteenth century.[3] Even today, in relatively advanced countries we can still find capital punishment, the beating of children by their parents and others, homeless people dying in the streets, and few who care. Bleeding hearts and do-gooders remain the objects of sarcasm. The fact is that humanitarianism is of very recent origin, the conversion of mainstream Christianity to it is more recent still, and its future remains desperately precarious. No wonder people try to entrench it by claiming that there is an humanitarian God out there who will see to it that humanitarianism survives.

Unfortunately this move is ceasing to work. Even churchpeople themselves increasingly recognize that they are projecting.

Increasingly we acknowledge that it was *we* who invented our God, and we are responsible for updating him. Trying to update our God, we produce black theology, feminist theology and so on. But now the projection has become ironical: when we *know* we're doing it, it no longer works in the old way because we are not at heart realists any more.

So I conclude that we can no longer make moral realism work. As a way of expressing our sense of the importance of our values, it is no longer convincing, not even to us.

I'm saying: 'Our values matter a lot, but the old objectifying realistic idioms are not a good way of bringing home the point.' In the same way, our religious faith matters a lot, but the old objectifying realistic talk about a God out there is not a good way to bring home the point. Thus, there are a lot of people who think that if you are an anti-realist about morality/science/religion, then you must think it doesn't matter what is believed about morality/science/religion. But it is time those people learned better. I am a Christian humanitarian, and I think it is very important that we should all detest cruelty and try to banish it from our social relationships. But I am also saying that some old ways of promoting this moral cause can now be seen to be no good. Trying in the old manner to set morality up on high is actually *bad* for morality. We should therefore not try to persuade people that there is an eternal and invisible cosmic Law against cruelty, or that there is a spirit-standard in the sky measured against which every cruel deed is shown to be wrong, or that the wrongness of cruelty is self-evident to reason, or *anything* of that sort.

Such ways of speaking do not work any longer, and cannot convince people who can now see that the whole of our life is lived inside history and inside language. Every detail of religion, of morality, and of culture generally is subject to historical change. There is no point in trying to keep up the pretence that any of our religious and moral ideas are certified from somewhere outside history. It was a ludicrously misleading notion anyway, for all our moral and religious ideas and values are intimately bound up with the contingent details of our bodily constitution, our feelings, our needs and desires, our practices, our social relations and our history. A God out there and values out there, if they existed, would be utterly useless and unintelligible to us.

There is nothing to be gained by nostalgia for the old objectivism, which was in any case used only to justify arrogance, tyranny and cruelty. People are forgetful; they just do not recall how utterly hateful the old pre-humanitarian world was.

So let us recognize that our abhorrence of cruelty and our other humanitarian values represent a recent and purely human creative moral achievement. It belongs within a certain context in the history of institutions, the history of ideas and the history of the emotions. A feat of the religious imagination was involved, as people began to direct towards their suffering fellow human being – including the child, the criminal, the lunatic, the woman, the black person – something of the ardent compassionate feeling which historically had been directed towards the suffering Christ. And people came to see the wretched of the earth as being like Christ in his sufferings in the very same period in which it also came to be believed that by public campaigning, legislation and so forth the burden of people's suffering could be very substantially reduced. The spirit of improvement, coupled with a movement to hominize Christianity, gave birth to our modern humanitarianism. Under these very special conditions a new cluster of values and a new ethical movement were forged; and to learn how utterly contingent it all was and still remains is, maybe, to be filled with determination to do one's bit to keep it going.

As for the question of justification, we may come to see the point of a new ethical movement in exactly the same way as we may come to see the point of any other new movement, in art or in culture more generally. We have to go over the arguments and the history, we have to feel the feelings and see the differences that are made to life – and then either we will see the point of a new value, or we will not.

4

VALUING OUR VALUES

From the point of view of Michel Foucault, the tone of the last chapters has been unduly overheated. We should not be surprised, and still less should we be indignant, at the uselessness of the past. As Foucault himself observes, in modern culture the matter upon which moral judgment is exercised – especially in face-to-face personal relations, and in matters of sex – is typically our feelings. We see it as important that we should liberate our desire and let our feelings run strong and true. We feel a strong moral need to live by the heart and be in touch with our own emotions, so that for us the standpoint for moral judgment must quite obviously be immanent; we must remain fully immersed in the biological flow of life. I would put it more strongly: for us morality is a matter of being true to the feel of life itself. Hence for us the best media for the exploration of questions of personal morality are the novel, drama, film and so forth, media in which we stay in time, narrative and the particular, because as we see it there could be no gain in moving to a passionless, universal and transcendent standpoint for moral judgment.

But, Foucault reminds us, ancient ethics was very different.[1] People aimed to be masterful and active, not passive; people aimed to achieve *self*-mastery; and for some there was the aim – uncommon in Christian times – of making one's own life as aesthetically beautiful as possible. When concerns like these are to the fore in your ethics, then the transcendent spectator's viewpoint – the view from above or outside – becomes very relevant. I shall *need* to transcend myself if I am to be able to govern myself or to assess my own life aesthetically.

Or again, take another case: Foucault points out that tradi-

tional Christian ethics was concerned with purity and immortality. Desire was thought of as instigated by Satan, and the keen
believer strove to quell his desires. Nowadays we are the exact
opposite: we go along to the doctor or the therapist to complain
about *loss* of libido. For us, vigorous sexual desire is no longer a
sign that we are fallen or that we are being attacked by Satan, but
a sign of positive health and well-being. When it fails we are in
trouble. As we see it, the attempt to mortify all our desires in
Christian asceticism was very badly misguided. But that is only to
say that our selfhood and our ethical style is quite different from
that of earlier times. We cannot say that we are right and they
were wrong; only that we are different from them.

Foucault stresses that a consequence of his analysis is that the
moralities of earlier times have nothing to teach us; and this is
true even though the rule-code may look much the same. For the
greatest changes take place in the way the self is constituted as a
moral subject, and in what is judged important in morality. Thus
it has often been pointed out that the early Christian moral code
was, *as code*, much the same as the Stoic code; but Foucault is
able to demonstrate how profoundly the Christian self as an
ethical subject differed from the Stoic self.

Foucault at the end of his career was much occupied in
reinventing ethics. He set aside the traditional and rather less
interesting topics of descriptive morals (how people in fact
behave) and moral code (the socially established rules of behaviour and evaluations of behaviours), and he used the term
'ethics' for the self's relationship with itself, *rapport à soi*; that is,
the way it constitutes itself, is aware of itself and functions as a
moral subject. There are four topics to be considered. The first,
substance éthique, is the aspect of the self and its life that is
especially singled out for moral assessment. It may be our acts,
our desires, our intentions, our public reputation or whatever.
The second, *mode d'assujettissement*, concerns the mode of
ethical motivation, or the manner in which moral obligation is
imposed upon the self. It may be as divine law, as natural law, as
rational principle, as aesthetic requirement and so on. The third,
pratique de soi, concerns the varied techniques of self-discipline,
self-examination, diary-keeping and so forth by which we
sharpen ourselves up as moral subjects. Finally, *téléologie* is
about what kind of self we are aiming to be. Again, there have

been various answers over the past twenty-five centuries: people have in different epochs sought public esteem, mastery, beauty, purity and immortality, freedom, and emotional harmony and maturity.

Thus redefined, ethics coincides with what I have elsewhere called 'spirituality': the varied forms of consciousness, the styles of selfhood. Foucault's analyses bring out how profoundly different the self has been at different periods in the past. He would certainly say that we have been wasting our time by even so much as troubling to complain about the ethics of Plato and classical Christianity. He says flatly in a 1983 interview that 'there is no exemplary value in a period that is not our period . . . it is not anything to get back to'.[2] If we want a Christian ethics for now, we have got to invent it now. The Christian moralities of the past can be of no use to us, and we should not be at all surprised by their utter foreignness. If we want to write a modern Christian ethics we may well learn much from D. H. Lawrence, but we can learn nothing from Augustine. His ethics – his form of ethical selfhood – is too different from ours. To resume an example that I have already quoted and which I think can now be understood more clearly, to Augustine, *Love your neighbour!* means, 'Perform some corporal works of mercy in order to purify your own soul thereby'. It certainly did not mean, 'Let your neighbour become your love-object', because for Augustine (as for Benedict, and for many another like them) Satan attacks us through the passions, and emotional involvement with a fellow human being is a serious threat to our chances of salvation.

Augustine's whole ideology links the passions with the flesh, corruption, suffering, time and loss of presence, the scattering of the soul. By contrast, he associates salvation with immortality, changelessness and passionlessness. The more we read him, the more we see the utter impossibility of our being *his* sort of self today. We live after the people of feeling: to quote typical early figures, Wordsworth, Schubert, Schleiermacher. We just cannot see the good life as a life from which desire has been eradicated and which is therefore without any warm human feeling except in the relation to God. (Augustine speaks so movingly and warmly to God that we are liable to forget that for him such warmth and intimacy was possible only in the relation to God. To be thus passionate towards a fellow human being would rot your soul.)

We have to put this plainly: a modern Christian ethic can only be had if we utterly forget pre-Enlightenment Christianity. *Our* ethics will be an ethics of the flesh, an ethics of human feeling, an ethics of libido and of being true to the life-energy in us. We will dress it up as being incarnational and as Christian humanism, and this will give it the necessary appearance of continuity. But it is merely 'the appearance', for the truth is that we can today be Christians only at the price of saying that there wasn't any Christianity to speak of before the later eighteenth century, and certainly none of any interest or relevance to us. The earlier religion was a power-structure and a kind of ritualized platonism, other-worldly, radically anti-human and anti-life. There is though one thing to be said in its favour: in the figure of Christ it retained a frozen image of the human, suffering, naked, glorious, which one day would be democratized and dispersed so that we might all come to feel, about each other, like *that*. For over seventeen centuries Christianity was transmitted in a time-capsule, in a state of suspended animation. Now we can thaw it out and bring it to life.

But we have a problem. We seek a modern Christian humanist ethics. We say that it has to be an ethics of life and feeling. But our project confronts a very serious split in the culture, roughly between mechanism and romanticism over the fact-value issue. One half of our culture says that valuation is, and is necessarily, omnipresent in our experience; but the other half seems to go beyond even Plato in stripping of value not merely the physical world but also, to a great extent, the self.

The first line of thought, about the omnipresence of valuation, comes from the Romantics and from modern biology. We are biological organisms, motile and living in time. Every smallest difference or change in ourselves or our environment may have a bearing upon our own well-being. So it is important to us that we shall very finely discriminate and evaluate what goes on in us and around us – and *therefore* we have sense organs and we develop beliefs and knowledge systems. Our world is made out of our valuations. Our sense organs are not neutral recording instruments, and our knowledge systems are not (so-to-say) 'exact copies' of reality – whatever *that* might mean. There would be no point in 'absolute' sense-experience and knowledge, and they are not in fact even conceivable. Necessarily, a biological being has an *interest*, its every sense-experience being a positive or a negative response of its own living sensibility to some impingement upon it. Without a differential feeling-response there would be no sense-experience, just as without a differential checking-out of how various beliefs work in relation to our life-interest there could be no knowledge. So from the biological point of view all of our active life is at bottom evaluative and every discrimination we are able to make is in the end an evaluative discrimination. As active process all life is evaluation, because there is no biological reason why we should ever have developed the ability to register *anything*, unless it directly affects our life-interest.

The other and contrasting line of thought stems largely from René Descartes and from the supposed value-neutrality, both of physical science as an activity, and of the mechanical world it constructs. Before Descartes it was just about universally held that if we are to come to the knowledge of the Real Truth, we must first make ourselves morally fit for it. Tradition prescribed a work we must perform upon ourselves, a discipline or an *ascesis* that we must follow in order to make ourselves into purified selves ready for Truth. Before Descartes, religion and ethics were greatly concerned with this *pratique de soi*. But Descartes, extraordinarily, establishes the self straight off by a kind of ontological argument. I think, therefore I am. He makes the self itself, straight off, the only founder of its own practices of knowledge. He eliminates the *pratique de soi* as irrelevant, because the really important and powerful truth is the truth that is evident to any attentive self, whether ethically purified or not. And finally, therefore, Descartes more radically eliminates the ethical than any other thinker before him, because he makes truth dependent only on the objective evidence of its presentation to the knower, and not at all upon the moral condition *of* the knower. Thus Descartes was the real founder of modern science as an institutionalized presence in society.

Descartes is thereby also the founder of a tradition for which value has become a problem. The world is value-neutral and the path to knowledge is value-neutral. Our value-judgments are not testable by the scientific method. What can their status be? It begins to look as if values are not objective constituents of the world at all, but are merely attitudinal and persuasive.

For Cartesian-mechanistic science, value is nowhere; for thoroughgoing biological naturalism, and in general for any immanent, 'Romantic' and life-centred outlook, value is everywhere. That is the puzzle. There are plenty of further complications, such as for example the problem of reflexivity that arises in connection with any statement of the ethics of life. (Do we claim theoretical truth for the statement, or is it itself an evaluation?) But the main collision is sufficient for now: are values real constituents of the world or not? Is every observation always an evaluation, and if it *is*, how do we account for the success of the Cartesian-mechanistic approach?

The general lines of the solution we propose are obvious enough. All the language that we use in the *lebenswelt* (the world of everyday life, as distinct from the world of the laboratory and the scientific paper) is thoroughly permeated with evaluations. I have argued elsewhere, and will not repeat the argument here, that the meaning of a word just is its felt position on some evaluative scale or combination of scales. Necessarily, as living agents with needs and desires, we see the world as having or lacking what we want, as friend or foe, bane or blessing. We swallow or we spit out; we like it, hate it or lump it, and these differential evaluative responses are the raw materials of knowledge. Only a biological being with a felt interest in life can have a sensibility, and its evaluative feeling-response to events taking place in its sensibility just *is* (via language) its cognition of the world.

We know by valuing, and we can know and value only because we are alive. A meter has no sense-experience, and an encyclopaedia doesn't know a thing. There is no absolute or objective knowledge or value in the strong metaphysical sense, because values are relative to our needs and desires and so also is knowledge. There is nothing odd about this, for what after all could be the *point* of purely objective truths and values subsisting out of any relation to our needs? Value can be conceived only as value-to and value-for, and knowledge has to be someone's knowledge.

Now if the life-world is at every point always seen in terms of values, if valuation is first of all, then values do not need objective grounding. Rather we should get to work on the valuations we are already making. They may be assessed and criticized, or in various ways selectively developed, trained and redirected. This too has already happened, for not only are the values of life always already in place but also we are always already within a *culture*, that is an organization and a transformation of the values of life. History has already bequeathed to us, embodied in our current language and practices, an interpretation of life or a second-level evaluation of life.

When all this is understood then ethical thinking becomes critical, because we see now that we are not trying to justify either morality in general or any particular morality, and we are not attempting to smuggle values into a human world that lacks them. Value is there already, culture is there already, a code is there already, and the task is to criticize, to re-interpret and to re-assess what we already have.

How then is Cartesian-mechanistic value neutrality and sci-entific realism possible? How does it, or did it, work? The basic reason is that at the most elementary level our valuations, coded as verbal skills, are held with a staggeringly high degree of unanimity. To see this, browse for a few hours in the English dictionary. Meditate on the fact that those lexicographers already know *exactly* what we know, but even better than we know it ourselves. Where words are concerned we all have near-perfect pitch. We are socially trained to be supersensitive to evaluative flavours or tones and their correlated words and verbal forms. You are now show-ing that supersensitivity, just by your skill in reading these lines.

So then, at the micro-level of valuation where words and verbal forms are correlated with felt social situations, sense-experiences etc., our evaluational feelings are extremely refined and drilled into such unanimity that like the music of the spheres they may pass unnoticed because they are so equably omnipresent. The unani-mity is so great that we seem to ourselves to inhabit a common, objective and even value-neutral physical world. Ordinary lan-guage of course already contains a cosmology (conceptions of space, time, matter, energy, causation, the self and so on) for science to polish up. Thus the prevalence and the plausibility of scientific realism is not surprising, and quite compatible with the point of view that we are putting forward.

Although at the micro-level of valuation we are in effect unani-mous, there is also a gross level of political, ethnic and religious divergence at which sharp value-conflicts arise. This conflict is the chief factor prompting us to attempt a revaluation of our values. In the older moral philosophy you defended what was more-or-less the morality of your own group, and you might even talk as if there was and could be only one truly moral morality and you were its advocate. But when moral philosophy grasps that there really *is* moral diversity, moral pluralism, *then* we can raise the question of a valuation of our values and a critique of moralities as such.

How is a revaluation of our values possible? What can be the moral standpoint for a moral critique of moralities? When it was first raised this question seemed impossibly paradoxical. Today we have got a little further with it and are able to distinguish a number of different lines of attack.

1. Traditionally, one pointed out that people don't live up to their professed ideals. That is banal enough, but in a few cases the observation amounts in effect to a telling criticism of the ideals themselves. They may be exposed as unworkable and perhaps impossibly high-flown.

2. Secondly, one may find an internal contradiction in a moral code, or set of practices, or set of valuations. This also is more interesting than at first appears, because our received moral beliefs, like our received religious beliefs, are often breathtakingly irrational and yet so entrenched that it is very difficult for us to perceive their irrationality. Society has limitless power to make absurd customs and beliefs seem sensible. An example: for three centuries an Englishman marrying said, 'With all my worldly goods I thee endow' – and thereby became the sole legal owner of all his wife's worldly goods. The performative that the groom uttered was the exact opposite of the legal effect of the rite – and what is interesting is the fact that until the nineteenth century nobody perceived the anomaly. Similarly, we can surely say with equal confidence that during the same period nobody was puzzled to notice that at a wedding the woman was both given away by her male guardian and made an autonomous promise to marry on her own behalf.

Cases like these suggest that moral systems can contain major but well-shielded inconsistencies that become apparent only when cultural change suddenly and unexpectedly exposes them. But if it is the case that we can for centuries be quite unable to recognize glaring inconsistencies in our own morality, then our *consciousness* of our own morality must be at a much lower level than we suppose. We think we know what we believe and what are our values, but we do not. Our official creeds and codes don't epitomize but function rather to *veil* our real faith, which is very odd.

3. That leads us to our third approach to a moral critique of morality. Our entire moral and religious tradition is so old and confused, and the contrast in it between the manifest and the latent is so marked, that we have a pressing need for a good deal of icy cold history of the sort that Foucault pioneered. For every moral and religious concept we need to ask questions of the *cui bono?* type. Why was this concept introduced, what part does it play in institutional life and power relations? . . . and so on.

4. It is also possible to carry out an immanent critique of a moral or religious position. Kierkegaard gives the best statement of the problem and of its solution. There are various distinct forms of consciousness, various moral and religious worlds that a person may inhabit, and there is no neutral standpoint for arbitration between them. So we cannot hope to prove, in the old foundationalist manner, that one view only is just true and all the others are just false. But we need not feel defeated. It is still possible to step imaginatively into somebody else's thought-world or circle of beliefs and values, and explore it from within. A novelist, a dramatist or a film-maker may do this so thoroughly that we feel she has equipped us to choose, rationally, whether we wish to make that world our world or not.

5. The fifth method of moral criticism of morality is the sniper's method. An agile critic may take a stand upon some part of a moral system and in terms of it criticize the rest, and then he can begin to move around like a sniper, firing at different targets from different angles. Eventually he will even shoot at his own former perch.

Tolstoy considered that an author should have a fixed and clear moral standpoint. (Hence his well-known reproof to Chekhov: 'Your plays are even worse than Shakespeare's.') But in recent English comic fiction the author is often found to use the sniper's method. He moves around cheerfully distributing ridicule in all directions, abusing both liberals from a reactionary point of view and reactionaries from a liberal. In a moralistic mood I once taxed David Lodge with being a sniper of this type. He was not pleased, and I see now that I should rather have congratulated him. A particular moral polarity like that between conservatives and liberals may become old, stale and boring. The sniper's method may help us to transcend it with laughter and so open up something new. (Much in morality is neither right-or-wrong nor true-or-false, but lively and usable or flat and unusable.) It is worth saying, and is a matter of some consequence, that there are themes in the received Christian morality that are admirable, innocent, worthy – and fatally, hopelessly dowdy. Are we yet ready for the idea that moralities need to be sharp and sexy, like fashions? We are certainly not. But we will need to accept the idea, if we are to have an ethics of life.

6. Finally there is the attack by ethical naturalism upon the very way morality has commonly been set up. In line with its overall two-worlds dualism the platonic tradition defines morality by contrast with nature, thus giving rise to a whole series of familiar distinctions. Inclination, the passions and life are opposed to duty, conscience and the moral demand. Is and ought, actual and ideal, indicative and imperative, hypothetical and categorical are all contrasted with each other. The ethical is portrayed as from-above, as unconditionally necessary and as having the authority always to overrule the needs and claims of life. It transcends the world of fact as God does.

We have suggested already that one difficulty with this scheme is that it seems to picture the moral realm as being both more real (because of its final and overriding authority) and yet also *less* real than the natural realm (because it is only ideal, and needs to be actualized). But another and perhaps more serious difficulty is that where morality is *defined* in terms of its opposition to life there can be no integration of the self and no general mediation between morality and nature, between the world of ideal value and the world of contingent fact. The traditional is-ought dualism implies that the self had got to stay split for ever and the world has got to stay split for ever. If the split were healed morality would disappear and value would disappear. The very spring of morality has been thought to consist in a certain tension and indeed an obdurate *antagonism* between is and ought, just as for the dualist the spring of religion is the tension and indeed *antagonism* between God and man (for just as a little spice of antipathy is needed to make the woman-man relation sexy, so a little spice of antipathy brings the relation between God and the soul to life).

In Kant's philosophy all these old philosophical dualisms, first set up by Plato, had become quite exceptionally prominent and clear-cut. Hegel protested, his philosophy of mediation being an application of the Christian themes of redemption and reconciliation to the traditional dualities. But Hegel's philosophy was dialectical, that is, he too begins by positing the dualities in order next to mediate between them, rather as Christianity keeps the Old Testament alongside the New. The Old Testament disjunction between the holy and the common is kept, in the background, in order to give force and point to the New Testament's synthesis of them.

By keeping the oppositions at least as a moment in the dialectical unfolding of his philosophy, Hegel thus drew attention to the way Christianity had done the same. Indeed, by his criteria medieval Christianity had been so dualistic as to have been closer in its religious type to the priestly tradition in the Old Testament than it was to the New Testament. And once we have understood Hegel's philosophy of mediation and his dialectical humanism we are bound to ask ourselves: Why did Christianity fall back and fail to complete its own project? Why is it a half-finished faith? Why did it never fully overcome the objective God-over-against-man, and why did it never fully believe in the plenary Incarnation of God in man? According to orthodox doctrine, in Christ the two natures divine and human lie side-by-side, conjoined indeed but still distinct and unconfused so that the infinite difference between the divine and the human remains unaltered. In the standard doctrine of the Incarnation, amazingly, God and man remain as far apart as ever. No true redemption, in the strong sense of a full and final *merger*, has taken place. Until roughly the period of Blake and Feuerbach, Christianity always lacked the courage to become itself. It stopped half-way, and this means that the is-ought distinction in ethics appears in Christianity in a peculiarly horrible and graphically-mythologized form, as the opposition between holy God and sinful man. Notoriously, the crushing way in which the language is deployed in this area robs us and our life of all value. It makes us hateful to ourselves and to each other, and has sometimes rendered Christians weak, guilt-ridden, vicious and psychopathic.

So there has been a protest. Ethical naturalism of the biological sort that became popular after Darwin (Nietzsche, Freud, Lawrence, etc.) attacks the values of otherworldly religion as alienated, decadent and sick. It praises life, the body, the passions and good health, and it denounces every sort of ethical idealism which attempts to remove value to an ideal world outside life. It usually rejects deontological ethics (that is, moralities based on the primacy of obligation) and the is-ought distinction outright, as tending towards otherworldliness, and instead seeks to make the distinction between good and bad entirely within life. This means that good is likely to be equated with health, maturity, vigour, purity and strength of feeling, etc., and bad with sickness, decadence, malfunction, festering and the like. And undoubtedly this *medicalizing* of morality creates problems. Over the millennia we had become habituated to the notion that a true moral judgment upon life has to be passed from a standpoint outside life by the application to life of life-transcending and timeless standards. The mythical, religious version of this idea was the doctrine of a Last Judgment. A very considerable shift in language is called for if we are to accept the thought that life has no outside, and that all our moral judgments have to be made within life and from the standpoint of life. But just to medicalize the language of morality as Nietzsche and so many others subsequently have done, just to shift control of the metaphoric from the priest to the doctor is, I am bound to say, rather feeble. Rabbitting on about health and maturity is not good enough. I have suggested that to develop a satisfactory ethics of life we will need to recognize that valuation is already omnipresent in life. Every fact, every sense-datum is already an evaluation . . . and so on.

The six methods of moral criticism that we reviewed indicate, I hope, that an evaluation of our values, a moral critique of our own morality, is not so impossibly paradoxical an undertaking as might at first appear. If it were indeed the case that there is and there can be only one truly moral morality, then indeed morality would be totalitarian. It would be logically impossible to get any leverage against it. There would by definition be no standpoint from which moral criticism could be brought to bear upon it. But at the opposite extreme, it is surely very hard to imagine how there could be two wholly discontinuous moralities with no common values whatever. If they really were utterly discontinuous, they couldn't be compared. In practice what we find is surely what the present discussion has suggested we will find, namely that there is a good deal of overlap among moralities. They may be more socialist or more individualist, more this-worldly or more other-worldly, more traditional or more creationist. But insofar as they all get coded into the same vernacular language, they all have to operate against the same background, namely the micro-level valuation of life that is acquired with language and is built into it. So as well as the manifest divergence between moralities there is also the micro-level background and the common language, which must operate to ensure at least some degree of overlap. It is this mixture of divergence and overlap which makes the moral criticism of moralities possible.

5

REMAKING THE CHRISTIAN SELF

(a) Biological Naturalism

Many people recognize that if the Christian tradition is not just slowly to fossilize but to be given a new lease of life, then its belief-system must be completely desupernaturalized. All reference to any supernatural world or beings or forces must be expunged or, at the very least, given a purely natural interpretation in terms of the way such talk shapes life here and how. Thus God, the heavenly world, life after death, Grace, answers to prayer, miracles and particular providences must be dialectically transformed or reinterpreted or whatever. All remaining traces of occultism and nostalgia for the old pre-scientific cosmology must go.

So far so good, but then there's a temptation to stop at that point, as if the ethics and the spirituality could remain relatively unaltered. That is not so, for as I have been suggesting we must also desupernaturalize Christian ethics and spirituality and, more fundamentally, the very form of Christian selfhood. The Christian psychology has to be humanized, so that we no longer fly off into a meagre, warped imaginary world in which we pretend that there is a kind of love that is 'higher' than real human love and a kind of justice 'higher' than human political justice. As Camus and Bonhoeffer both put it (independently, I think) almost half a century ago, we must give up the childish fantasy of becoming saints in favour of the altogether loftier, more demanding and nobler task of becoming human beings.

Nor is this false rhetoric. Over the past twenty-five years hundreds of people have left the celibate priesthood or the religious orders of women in order to be laicized and in due course to marry. I have known perhaps a dozen such people personally, and many of them have also written their autobiographies. Without exception, it seems, they report wonder and gratitude at the solid moral reality and happiness they have found in the common human experience of marriage and sex and babies. After the overheated illusions of the 'religious life' with its merely metaphorical 'marriage', the real thing has the impact on them of a religious conversion. Such people are fortunate, because they have experienced the full imaginative shock of an incarnational and secularized Christianity. While they were young and ardent they were trained in the old supernaturalism. They really believed it; and then all that religious feeling which had been evoked and directed up towards heavenly objects was returned to earth and resolved down into its human basis. They experienced an Hegelian synthesis as Spirit became flesh, agape became eros, and the Holy Family became their own human family. This was the natural supernaturalism of which Thomas Carlyle spoke, over a century ago, and it is an indication of the route along which we may be able to get some moral reality, some truth, and some imaginative force back into Christianity – if only we can secularize it hard enough.

Our immediate task is to secularize and humanize the Christian self, in particular by absorbing the implications of modern biological naturalism. This is not quite so simple a matter as it may seem. Although in religious circles there is endless reiteration of stock – and largely incomprehensible – formulae such as 'God made us' (and 'in his own image', to boot) there is also a sense in which it has always been perfectly well understood that human beings are animals. We must not suppose that Darwinism suddenly changed everything. On the contrary, the deep affinity between man and beast has been a commonplace, probably, ever since animals were first domesticated. The very detailed analogies and homologies in body structure, physiology, behaviour and so on could not be missed. Animals came to play a very prominent part in myth, religion and art, and have been stock moral emblems and the subject of countless folktales.

The very closeness of man and animal prompts speculation about the difference between them, and traditional thought always tends to attribute a difference to the presence or absence of a thing. So, to put it in the form of an equation, man − animal = soul. However, man − corpse = soul, also. Are we to conclude that an animal is equivalent to a corpse? No: that cannot be right for, animal − carcass = animal soul. So an animal is made alive by its animal soul, and a human being is made alive by having a human soul, and the difference between a human being and an animal boils down to the difference between a human soul and an animal soul. An animal's soul is the principle of its sentience and motility. We have those powers too, but we also have some extra capacities. So, human soul − animal soul = speech, reason, conscience and immortality.

Traditional thought, then, regards a human being as an animal with an extra-high-powered type of soul. The distinctively human capacities were seen in Christian thought as supernatural, in a limited sense, for each immortal, rational human soul is specially created by God, whereas animal souls are not. They are just propagated by natural generation.

Now one of the most important functions of culture is to recognize and then symbolically to enhance and elaborate the basic cosmological distinctions that are of the most importance to human life. One such distinction is, for example, the man-woman distinction. There are a number of biological differences between men and women, but culture for its own purposes dramatically hypes them up and exaggerates them. One reason for this is intellectual: hyped-up and metaphorically-enriched by culture, the man-woman relation becomes a cognitively-important paradigm case of binary distinction. It helps us to generate, and it provides us with interpretative metaphors for, thousands of other differences.

Of all the basic cosmological distinctions the most important to culture is the one that secures culture itself, namely the distinction between culture and nature. And *of* the culture-nature distinction, the man-beast distinction is itself a concentrated epitome and a natural symbol. Broadly, one could put the point like this: we've got to get the man-animal distinction right because on it hinges our very identity as human beings. Thus we may expect to find that culture ascribes very high prestige or 'holiness' to that in human beings which is distinctive and non-animal. Often culture will set out to enhance our sense of the distinctively human by requiring us to repress everything in ourselves that is animal, bestial or brutish. Women, it seems, are required to repress the animal in themselves more strongly than men are. Boys are almost encouraged to be grubby, aggressive scapegraces, whereas girls have to be well-groomed, to conceal perfectly ordinary biological functions, and to remove body hair that grows in the wrong places. The contrast between grubby boy and extra-spruce girl is a sign of the cultural task of women.

The most highly-regarded human life will in this context be the least animal. What do animals enjoy most? Freedom, alert senses, the hunt, the kill, food, sociable grooming, courtship, mating, nesting, raising young and lazy sleep in times of plenty. Now imagine a way of life in which every single one of these basic animal pleasures has been either repressed as far as possible or cut out altogether. It will be a way of life characterized by vows of obedience, mortification of the senses, restrictions on movement, seclusion, fasting, celibacy, vigils and so on. In short, it will be *precisely* the way of life of an enclosed contemplative nun. In the context of the traditional type of thought that prevailed in Europe from the fourth century to the seventeenth, the enclosed contemplative life thus had an important social function. It had little to do with Christianity. Rather, by so ruthlessly repressing the animal it bore symbolic witness to the distinctively human. Today we are likely to see the enclosed contemplative as a tragic and disturbed figure, but in the context of that traditional thought-world he or she was the highest human type. Woman − animal = nun.

Thus we explain the paradox that in a culture that knew perfectly well that 'man is a rational animal' the most highly-admired way of life was systematically and ruthlessly anti-biological. Even after the great age of the monastic ethic had come to an end, the old anti-biological emphasis persisted in an internalized form in Protestant ethics. A Protestant showed his difference from the merely animal by his cleanliness, hard work and self-discipline. His will was strong and his principles were firm. He kept strict control over his own bodily integrity and his emotions. He regarded animals as being much like Roman Catholics, but still more so. They were shamelessly demonstrative and lacking in self-control. They were prone to making an exhibition of themselves and needed to be kept on a short leash. Animals were dirty dogs, indifferent to pollution. Often you had to look away, embarrassed at what they got up to.

Although the Protestant – hilariously portrayed in his latest, Kantian, form in Michel Tournier's novel on the Robinson Crusoe theme – has rather comically psychologized the old values, he nevertheless still represents a supernaturalism of reason and the moral will that derives from Plato. A human being is a Jekyll and Hyde, a two-part creature. The higher spiritual nature should master the lower nature and whip it into obedience, as a horseman breaks and trains his horse.

The story of the slow disintegration of this ancient conception of the self and its moral struggle is very familiar. In the heyday of the Enlightenment figures like Hume and Gibbon argued that the 'monkish virtues' were in fact anti-social and unappealing. Their pursuit led to the decay of public spirit and the fall of civilization. The first thinker to put forward a thoroughly biological view of human nature (and he was justly proud of his own originality in this respect) was, however, Schopenhauer. Unfortunately Schopenhauer himself was psychologically scarred and not cut out for happiness. So he oddly combined the movement to biological naturalism in his philosophy of human nature with a very depressing neo-ascetical ethic. After him Darwin quickly made full historical continuity between animals and humans undeniable, and made a sound beginning on the task of explaining human reason, morality and religion up from below. Able people like Nietzsche and Freud who read Darwin in their teens saw at once that he had opened the way to a fully 'bottom-up' and naturalistic understanding of the mind. Whatever the residual difficulties, we all know in our hearts that the old Platonic supernaturalism of reason and morality and the old soul-body dualism are now dead beyond recall.

Of course culture can and does considerably transform nature. But what can be the point, we now ask ourselves, of practices and objectives in morality and religion that are contrabiological, that are biologically impossible, that seek to repress the biological drives or to pretend that they can be wholly left behind? To Darwin and to most of us since him, it is obvious that many ascetical practices are not only irrational and impossible of success but are also emotionally ambiguous and dubious. Furthermore, in our culture as it has now developed we have every reason to think that sin and guilt are a waste of time. They do no good. People who are at ease with themselves are of much more use to society than are people who hate themselves, and children who are loved and encouraged do better than children who are made to feel unworthy and bad. We should forget about sin, guilt and self-conquest, and concentrate on being kind to each other instead: the results will be far better.

In the next two generations after Darwin a number of key figures worked on the reconstruction of the West's moral psychology. Interestingly the majority of them were not in fact orthodox Darwinians, but they were all fully apprised of the importance of the new biological naturalism. They include Nietzsche, William James, Freud, Bergson, D. H. Lawrence, G. B. Shaw and Albert Schweitzer, and between them they have brought about a considerable change in our psychology. This in turn makes it possible for us to see at least the main headings for the future revision of Christian ethics. They are a group of interconnected ideas.

1. Christian ethics can no longer encourage resignation and the indefinite postponement of personal happiness and fulfilment – even, as so often in the past, until after death. On the contrary a religious ethic has got to help us to say Yes to life now.

2. The old supernaturalism of reason, conscience and the will led people in the past to think that because these things are distinctively human, the most fulfilled human life would consist of *nothing but* the pure intellectual contemplation of absolute perfection. By our logical standards there is an obvious fallacy in this, and in any case moderns tend to object strongly to the reification of reason, conscience and the will. At least since the seventeenth century confessors have been aware of the danger of excessive scrupulosity, and we all now recognize that for every person who is morally too slack there is another who is morally too intropunitive and too much debilitated by feelings of unworthiness and self-doubt, and a third who is emotionally damaged by a 'will' that is too hard-driving and demanding. As a result of these psychological commonplaces we no longer find helpful the old model of practical reason (reason/will/conscience) governing the passions. It is better to see 'reason' and 'conscience' as just a certain cultural ordering of the passions, and to picture the path to well-being as a quest for emotional integrity, maturity, harmony, health, sincerity, balance or fulfilment. Too many words and too vague, but they express our more natural-

istic understanding of the self as a dynamic system of emotions. If our feelings run strong and true and if we are able to express them in our relationships, then that is half the battle. At least by approaching the matter from this angle we will be less likely to reify reason and conscience, and that is important because where they *are* reified the personality comes out warped and malformed.

I go further. Without repeating in full an argument already given elsewhere, I maintain that there are no such 'things' as reason, conscience, the will, the contemplative life and so on. We are bundles of life-energy. Living, we quiver with our continual sensitive, evaluative feeling-response. Events in our life are ripples, criss-crossing and running over the body surface. A meaning is just a cultural scaling of a ripple. Logic and syntax are just patterns in the movement of the body forces that have been abstracted and canonized by culture. There's nothing 'supernatural' about pure thought. A 'thinker' is just a person who makes up sentences, a sentence is a syntagmatic chain of signs running over the body surface, and the chain is in turn just a micro-procession of delicately-nuanced feelings through which a quantum of life-energy is expended.

If all this is so, if it is the case that the so-called 'loftiest' spiritual, moral and artistic achievements are just culturally-guided readings of the play of biological feeling, *then* those post-Freudians are right who say that our first task is always to recognize and to come to terms with our own emotions. And we need to break with the long philosophical and religious tradition of downgrading the body and the emotions, as if we supposed that our moral and spiritual life could somehow do without them altogether.

3. An obvious corollary is that we reject any supernaturalist account of *agapé*, Christian love, such as was given by the Lutheran writer Anders Nygren.[1] Agapé is just ordinary human affection and compassion, such as will flow freely if we can but become liberated from self-concern and its attendant anxieties.

The reason why agapé is spoken of (metaphorically) as supernatural is that it has the power to counteract 'the logic of division' whereby every distinction we make tends to give rise to discrimination and so to oppression. All human judgment, we maintain, is at bottom evaluative; and we make the world knowable by carving it up, that is, by making distinctions. Thus we distinguish light from darkness, land from sea, animal from plant, sun from moon and so on. In each of these cases we are able to make the distinction because culture has taught us to read in a value-difference. The first member of the pair is seen as the more normal, dominant, selfsame, upright and masculine. The second in each case is its subordinated other, its feminine counterpart, and is slightly aberrant.

Now, in the same way, every human group identifies itself by distinguishing itself from those who are not of the group. Every *we* is formed by contrasting itself with a *they*. Again, *we* are normal, clean, upright and rational, whereas *they* are a bit strange, deviant, unclean and aberrant.

Thus every human group is in some degree racist, sexist, chauvinist, speciesist or otherwise exclusive and prejudiced against outsiders. Some moral energy is required in order to counteract this phenomenon, and Christian ethics calls it agapé. It is most typically manifest as a love and compassion that goes out to embrace the victims of social discrimination, underdogs of every kind. Since it is love for the Other, it is obviously at root sexual. This love justifies the ungodly and from our modern humanitarian standpoint is the essence of Christianity, shining out equally clearly in the Gospels and in modern struggles to defend the human rights of the downtrodden. But for most of Christian history the principle has been more honoured in the breach than in the observance. Agapé is supernatural, then, not in being asexual but in the sense that it runs counter to what would otherwise be an unchecked and universal human tendency.

4. Finally, as we have indicated already, in a revised Christian ethics pride of place must be given to creative, expressive, value-realizing human action. Everybody has a talent, everybody must be ambitious, everybody must make a contribution, everybody can *create* and everybody can be God in the sense of being an original, making the rules and creating values.

In a future Christian society everybody is going to be God, but the crucial point is to get the motivation right. Traditional Christian ethics did not applaud creative achievement, and gave it no official encouragement at all. You were not supposed to excel, except in penitence and self-abasement. It was – and in many quarters still is – conventional to disclaim ambition, and any Christian who by exceptional ability or industry won fame or high preferment had to profess astonishment, humility and reluctance at finding honours being thrust upon him. There seemed to be plenty of reasons for this charade. Human beings were weak and sinful, and you could do a good thing only insofar as God did it through you. Strictly, God alone did all good works and to God alone belonged the glory. Against that background creative drive was readily seen as motivated by a presumptuous lust for personal fame, power, wealth and advancement. This was not only highly sinful in itself but could be read as a very dangerous provocation, an attempt to rival God.

Historically, there just was no Christian ethics. You were too much afraid of attracting God's jealous wrath if you achieved anything. The idea instead was to work to rule and to concentrate on cleansing yourself. Before going to confession you worked your way through a very lengthy form of self-examination in order to identify all the sins you had committed. These you then confessed and obtained absolution for. That is, the aim was sin-reduction. You sought to make yourself as passively-conforming and perfectly inoffensive as possible. There was no *ethic*, because the whole grand system of psychological terrorism had no other purpose than to procure total submission to the power of God and the church. Christians have sought, and they can understand, humility, self-denial, obscurity, resignation, impotence and reliance on faith, but they scarcely yet know what to do with creative energy. I can personally testify that the old terroristic, corrupt, cosmic-protection-racket Christianity was still flourishing in the 1950s, because I was raised in it. The political Right have not yet given up their efforts to reinstate it. So the change is very recent and we are scarcely yet fully adjusted to it. We are still as likely to perpetuate old suspicions in modernized form as to renounce them, and the traditional Christian fear of action therefore lives on in the common suggestion that hard-working productive people are merely trying to expiate guilt and so to win a heterodox salvation by works.

Evidently, if we are to frame a Christian ethic of creative human action we must overcome or at least circumvent a number of old fears, including the fear that it may make God jealous and the fear that its motivation may be sinful. It is probably best to meet such fears head on. For there to be a Christian ethic, then, the old objective personal God must go and the old soul must go.

The old sort of God must go because he did everything, he had finished all the creative work already and he wouldn't let human beings truly invent any values or accomplish anything on their own. The old soul must go, because if we have ready-made customized immortal souls then there isn't any point in this-worldly action. Instead our only task is to get through this brief life without letting our souls become besmirched. If you already have a substantial individual immortal soul, you do not need to make history. Sin-reduction is quite enough. But if on the other hand I have no ready-made soul, if I am a process of becoming so that I shall just be the life I have led and no more, then I must try to live a full life and put a lot into it. The aim is not to make a big and lasting self, because there is no lasting self. Rather, I recognize that I am only one transient intersection in the human communications network. All that I shall have been is the contribution that I have been able to make to the whole communicative life of humanity. By making such a contribution I do my bit towards injecting value and meaning into human life and so keeping the show on the road. There is not and there cannot be any 'objective' meaningfulness or value, so that humanity is nothing but what each and all of us puts into it. But as we have sought to show, all human activity is creative. It has to be. It is evaluative, symbolic and meaning-making. Every smallest event that takes place in us, every least ripple in our sensibility, is a micro-evaluative response. In principle it is capable of being encoded by culture, turned into a symbol, read as a word, and so of being released into the network. Thus human life is creative and meaning-making through and through, and to strive to develop people's creativity is to strive for the fulfilment of their humanity.

(b) The Ethics of Self-Realization

Historically, views of the self have been many and extremely varied, and even seemingly-bizarre theories may still sometimes be revived. In tribal and pre-philosophical cultures belief in a plurality of souls was common, the ancient Egyptian, for example, having seven components of his whole person. This may seem a strange theory and unlikely ever to return; yet Robert Orstein has in fact lately introduced a plural, modular theory of the mind.[2] However, so far as present-day religious and philosophical thought are concerned the conceptions of the self that really count boil down to three.

The first is most splendidly exemplified in Augustine's *Soliloquies* and *Confessions*, where the self is seen as a 'centred', self-present, autonomous and sovereign spiritual Subject. The chief point to grasp is that God is the one and only real Self, because fully to live up to this conception of selfhood you need to be infinite and absolute or self-existent (*a se*). So God the Infinite Subject is the only completely and unalterably selfsame Self. You and I have been created by him to be his finite counterparts. Made by him for himself, we can become selves like him by his grace and by attending exclusively to him. Where this conception of the self is held, we are likely to find some kind of monasticism, and belief both in immortality and in 'recollection' or innate ideas, for it is held that the soul has *a priori* knowledge of the eternal world to which it belongs. We also find an erotic mysticism of I and Thou: the human soul is feminine and God is its Lord and Master. He penetrates the soul, infusing something of his own divinity into it.

The second doctrine of the self is that taught by the Buddha, Hume, Parfit and various recent French post-structuralists and 'anti-humanists'. The autonomous-spiritual-substance self is rejected as being illusory. The self is in truth nothing but a temporary aggregate of phenomena. There is no unchanging nucleus or core-self, no single continuing entity. Each overall state of the whole collection simply gives rise to the next. This no-self doctrine, it is claimed, liberates us from disabling egoism, anxiety and self-concern. The ethic that corresponds to it will typically be an ethic of non-attachment, disinterestedness, coolness, compassion, dispersal and self-loss.

Schopenhauer's endorsement gave Buddhism a bad name, and to this day some Westerners still describe it as suicidal and nihilistic. We can get a fairer view by comparing two visions of landscape. A Western landscape portrays a paradise lost and yet to come, with intense religious feeling; yearning after lost sexual innocence and happiness long ago, grief over sin, disobedience, banishment and exile, and longing to get back to the golden days. The vision of nature is weighed down with a heavy freight of emotion. By contrast, Oriental landscape is just beautiful in its evanescence, light and impressionistic, *unburdened*, that's all – and as the Buddhist sees landscape so he also sees his own self.

Both Augustine and the Buddha are pre-historical. Augustine aims to be pure, chaste and self-surrendered to God; the Buddha aims to be cool and free from the tyranny of the passions. Neither thinks for a moment of making history, and both reject desire. They are about equally different from the modern sort of self that appeared during the later eighteenth century, the expressivist, romantic, historical self. There were various strands in the making of this novel kind of person, of which the first is the doctrine of natural rights, used to push back the old absolutism of God and the King. A right is a limit on their power over the individual. By way of cutting down the pretensions of the earthly absolute monarch, it was claimed that God himself had chosen to operate as a constitutional monarch, conferring natural rights upon human beings at their creation before even the State arose. It was as if we were protected by a pre-existent and cosmic Bill of Rights, and this invocation of a primitive era before the State led also to the doctrine of autonomy. Under absolute rule people are like minors, but prior to the rise of the State and with nobody yet ordering them about, they must perforce have been morally autonomous. Their modern revolt against absolute monarchy is a clear sign that they are returning at last to their original adulthood.

So far we have the conception of the self as the subject of natural moral rights, and as an adult, autonomous and rational moral agent. The ethic is republican. Sovereignty has become de-centred, taken from the Monarch and distributed throughout the citizenry so that they can all come of age. God is perhaps a constitutional monarch now, and may certainly be seen as the presiding Ideal of Reason.[3] The civil law is regarded as an expression of reason, and we believe in freedom under the law. But to get to the Romantic self we need more yet. We have to break with the long-established habit of seeing the self as almost timeless, and children therefore as just solemn miniature adults. We need the doctrine of personal development that arrived with Herder, and the accompanying interest in psychology, in *Bildung* and in the life-cycle. Then it becomes possible to see the self as developing towards maturity through its own expressive activity. Selfhood becomes a task and a project, to be executed immanently (that is, by me, in my own strength, here and now and in my own life). I must strive, through my life and work in historical time, progressively to fulfil my capacities and so gradually to become the mature, unique self that I have it in me to be. There is no standard universal human *Telos*, but there is something that I and only I can become, and it's my task to become it.

In one form or another this doctrine is almost universal in the modern world, common to the headmaster and the drop-out. On speechday the headmaster declares that every child (*scilicet*, however dim) has it in her or him to make a contribution and to become something special, and it's the job of the school to bring it out. This sounds like the emergence of the finished sculpture from the rough-hewn block of marble, with school discipline knocking off the rough corners. The drop-out too wants to become an individual, but he does not want to be knocked into shape by the system. He demands absolute Bohemian freedom to become himself in his own way. The headmaster believes in society as the nursery of individuation, whereas the drop-out seems to believe in nature. The one is more socialist and the other more anarchist. But in other ways they are rather alike, for they are both close to a form of essentialism; that is, both conjure up the idea that there is out there ahead of me a pre-designed, essential, fully-individual Real Me. It is waiting out there for me to catch up with it, so that I become it and it finally gets itself actualized in me. The recipe for turning the present me into that future glorious Real Me may differ in the two cases, the headmaster being more like a settled monk and the drop-out more like a mendicant friar, but both of them are indebted to traditional ideas of pilgrimage, quest and vocation, and to the essentialist and teleological doctrine of a Real Self out there waiting for me to become it.

Ever since Plato, essentialism has postulated a parallel ghost-world that guides this world's course and acts as its goal. Romanticism's only change is that the ghosts have become more personalized, more individuated than they were in Plato. But essentialism remains a primitive and mythical idea. *Of course* there is no sense in the idea of a ready-made Real Me waiting out there for me to become it, a Real Me that is both realer than the current me because it's already out there authoritatively demanding that I become it, and less real than the current me because it is after all only ideal until I have actualized it by becoming it.

The essentialist doctrine is untenable. After we have recognized and dismissed it, what are we left with? – Something like the ancient sculptural metaphor. My life is an art-project. I have to become an individual, and in this task I am my own Pygmalion. Just what sort of work of art I may be able to make of my self and my life is in no way predetermined. We can, however, say with the headmaster that indeed social institutions should as far as possible be designed so that they don't force people into standard shapes, but encourage them to become and to treat each other as individuals. And we can say with the drop-out that he is right to be super-libertarian. The moral task of becoming a self and finding one's own voice is very like the artist's task of finding a distinctive personal style. To work your way through to something that is really your own demands a great deal of time, of freedom and of solitude. It also demands perhaps more self-discipline and a more minute care in one's relations with other people than the drop-out may realize.

The Romantic and idealist vision of our life as a project of self-realization has become a commonplace of the modern world, and has even been to a considerable extent adopted by Christianity. Nor is this surprising, because there always was a strong tradition of individualism in Christianity. In baptism, in conversion, in moral decision and in prayer the individual stands alone. Furthermore, in Europe Christianity and individualism are roughly coeval. The emergence of the individual is documented in the history of Greek sculpture. The earlier whole-body sculpture is universal and cosmic, its face smiling, peaceful or abstracted; but when in the fourth century BC the head is separated from the body and portrait sculpture begins, we are made aware of a centred, intense and often deeply troubled individual subjectivity engaging us through the eyes.[4] This Hellenistic subjectivity is in search of redemption, and it is going to become gnostic or Christian.

However, strong though the individualistic tradition in Christianity may be, it is sometimes uneasy with the doctrine that the self should be its own prime object of moral concern. We know that we should work out our own salvation with fear and trembling – but we quail a little before the sedulous self-absorption of the Me-generation, the Body Shops, and the sheer dandyism of many in the various minorities. Can something like *this* be the future of Christian ethics? The thought makes us feel just a little queasy.

The issue is often raised in Christian circles in the form of a dispute about the correct interpretation of a biblical saying attributed to both Moses and Jesus: 'You shall love your neighbour as yourself.' This saying can obviously be understood in different ways. It *could* be read as highly sarcastic, in tone a little like Luke 11.13 ('If you then, being evil, know how to give good gifts to your children . . .'). In that case its force would be: You are a rotten lot of egotists; can you even *imagine* what it might be like to start to care as much about other people as you all-too-evidently do about yourselves? However, virtually all modern interpretations of the saying betray the influence of the ethics of self-realization. At the very least, it is suggested, Jesus here acknowledges that there is indeed such a thing as self-love, that it's perfectly proper, and that we begin from it. The saying is not at all hostile to self-love. Rather, its purpose is to get self-love and neighbour-love into balance.

How does it do this? There are two interesting answers, one that comes from Kant and another that comes from Nietzsche and Jung. The Kantian interpretation enjoins us first to be strictly rational and impartial. Assess yourself as one subject of rights and duties among others. Look at yourself-among-others as if from the viewpoint of a disinterested ideal observer, and don't be either too hard on yourself or too soft on yourself. The only rational basis for any discrimination is the fact that we each of us have prime responsibility for our own conduct. You are directly morally accountable for yourself, so under the general rubric of equality each agent should strive for her own virtue and for other people's happiness. If everyone follows that maxim, we will make up a society of fully-benevolent moral individualists.

The other answer is to be found in Nietzsche and Jung. It might be called ideal egoism. Each of us has a spiritual task; our Higher Self is to come to birth in us. We are pregnant with the Self we are to become and we must carefully tend this precious burden. The reproach of 'egoism' is quite mistaken. As a matter of fact, if each person cared more about her or his own spiritual life we would all of us be a great deal kinder to each other, and less demanding and interfering.

Of these two interpretations Kant's is the more objective and public-spirited. Nietzsche and Jung perhaps betray a little of the introversion and self-preoccupation of the solitary thinker, concerned about his own inner development and his duty to make the most of his talent. And perhaps all forms of the ethic of self-realization are open to the criticism that they do not take death sufficiently seriously. The parallel with art leads them astray. The artist makes a work that he hopes may outlive him, but if the work of art in which I am trying to express myself is *myself* and my own life, then I work in a very transient medium. I am writing in water and the work melts away as I perform it. Or suppose that I am aiming to make a better future self: I knock myself out for fifty or sixty years laboriously trying to learn some kind of wisdom and to become a tolerably stable and equable character – and almost at once biology takes over and I begin my descent into oblivion. How can the ethics of self-realization come to terms with the sheer transience of the self?

At this point I am – believe it or not – sometimes attracted to frivolous dandyism: seriousness is ridiculous, be a butterfly, just live for the moment. The truly wise person is frivolous on principle and never thinks about death or about life as a whole, or about *anything* long-term. What we must avoid like the plague is the neurotic and quite incurable Pascalian gloom about the human lot which has led some people to feel that the whole of our life is as it were lived in the condemned cell awaiting execution. Anyone who spoke in those terms to Wittgenstein was rebuked sharply. Such thoughts poison life and should never be entertained at all. In this vein some Victorian agnostics used to read and quote Spinoza's rebuttal of Plato: the wise man's meditation is *not* of death, but of life.

A similar remedy is sought by all those who in a great variety of ways get rid of the countdown to extinction by seizing eternity or by achieving a full circle of time in the present moment. Schopenhauer says, Don't think you are a cork bobbing along, being carried away by the river of time. You are a rock standing up from the river. Time rushes past you but you yourself are always in the present, in a *nunc stans*. You are never anywhere else but in the present, and you will never know a present without you.[5] Kierkegaard says that the bird of the air lives in the present moment, but the Christian lives *eternally* in the present moment. Nietzsche says an ecstatically joyful Yes to the eternal recurrence, and Proust transcends time as it comes full circle for him and he regains the past in the present.

The entire idealist tradition in philosophy, from Hegel through to Bradley, McTaggart, Whitehead and Heidegger, abounds in interesting but lightweight ideas and suggestions such as these, all of them designed somehow to diminish the threat which time and death present to the ethics of self-realization. There would not have been so many suggestions if the problem were not acute, and there would not have had to be so *many* suggestions if any of them were any good. In a word, the ethics of self-realization, helped out by the fund of devices we call upon to ward off the thought and the power of death, is our modern form of paganism. It is touching, but there is something not quite grown-up about it.

Nowadays we do not need redemption from 'sin'. It is sufficient to forget 'sin', a word that was once very ugly but is now merely redundant. What we need to be redeemed from is meaningless-ness, and in particular the way time and death like waves on the sand relentlessly wash away any and every kind of barrier we try to erect against them.

Christianity promises redemption – though not, we must at once add, the barmy fantasy of 'life after death'. Until all wish-fulfilment notions of that sort have been abandoned it is quite impossible to grasp the true message of Christianity, which is that to conquer death we must before death die to death and to the self. *That* is redemption, and everything else that has been superadded is illusion and self-deception.

'Dying to death' means completely and consistently renounc-ing a certain conception of the self, *and also* certain ambitions. We have to give up the conception of the self as a substance that is or can be made finished and permanent. I am fleeting all through and something that was not fleeting wouldn't be me. I am incomplete and unfinished, and if I were to become finished in the sense of being finalized or perfected then I'd be finished in the popular sense: just *dead*. My subjective feeling of personal identity and continuity is a construct; it is very transient and irregular, and it links together a fairly disparate collection of desires, aims, roles and behaviours. Furthermore the various devices by which we try to boost the 'I', promising to remember it and so forth, are mere social fictions. Many of them are valuable social fictions and deserve to be supported, but it should not be pretended that they are more than they are or that they accomplish more than they do.

When I truly take in all this – it is called 'dying with Christ' – then that in me which fears death and is threatened by it gets dissolved away. As all the talk about Christ makes plain, the Christian pathway to self-realization is by self-emptying, *kenosis*. To become inwardly emptied-out is the only way to a pure love of life and of our neighbour. Post mortem, we are no longer under threat and value just pours into life. This is the much-talked-about redemption of the world: we give up 'the soul' and 'life after death'. We give up egoism and fantasies. And now ethics becomes possible, ethics in the sense of action that infuses value into life. When we have died to ourselves, we can create and redeem the world. When we have become nothing we have become gods.

(c) The Old Western Self

It's a cliché. Everybody is agreed that there is something wrong with the traditional Western Christian form of selfhood that has come down to us, ultimately, from Paul and Augustine. It believes in a gospel of forgiveness and Grace, but it doesn't act forgiven. Too often it is irritable, querulous, censorious, inhibited and depressive, excessively self-conscious, and apt to use moral blackmail in its tireless quest for moral superiority and spiritual power over others. The one thing it is *not* is relaxed and easy-going.

The whole psychology has recently been persuasively traced back to Paul, in whose texts passages joyously expressive of love and peace are interwoven with other passages in which the Apostle demands submission to his own authority and becomes insanely jealous at the news that some rival spiritual leader may be working in his territory. Paul can get along with completely loyal and docile colleagues, and might even be able to endure an independent operator whose teaching was exactly the same as his. But what he cannot stand is the thought that the members of his flock should be exposed to a teaching that differs ever so slightly from his own.

We have already suggested that one reason for all this tension is that there were severe internal ideological conflicts within Christianity from the outset. The theology is about power, a supreme power and authority that descends from God through Christ to the Apostles and most particularly to Paul. It is the power of an almighty and jealous Father who can brook no rival and tolerate no dissent – none whatever, not the slightest. It is the most thrilling of all forms of power, namely spiritual power, the keys of the kingdom and the power of salvation. The thought that the administration of power such as this may be delegated to human beings is sufficient to spark off a sharp struggle for legitimacy: I want a piece of this power, I want the legitimacy and plentitude of my authority to be unquestioned, I want submission and I want no rivals. At the same time, in order to magnify the greatness of this power an ideology develops which pictures ordinary human beings as sinful, weak, threatened by imminent damnation and in desperate need of divine forgiveness. Everything is inflated rhetorically to the highest pitch. God's holiness, power and glory and his abhorrence of deviance could not be greater. Our human peril and need of salvation could not be more utterly desperate. God's mercy and generosity in Christ are as unbounded as they are undeserved. The urgency, the adequacy and the saving efficacy of the Gospel are all as great as can be. Theology becomes competitive boosterism: the most orthodox teaching will be reckoned that which uses the most superlatives in exalting God and in vilifying our human nature.

After this it is no surprise to learn that Christ took care that there should be no mistake about the rights. He sewed up the whole thing; the Apostles have the exclusive franchise. They know the secret of what the product is, they control its distribution, they have juridical authority in all matters connected with it – and Paul is one of them. Don't you dare dispute it.

Now, however, Paul is caught in a paradox. More than any other leader of the early church known to us, he suffered from having his apostolic status and authority questioned. Accordingly, more than any other he asserts them. He inflates the ideology of the apostolate and his own personal legitimacy and authority, and furthermore he also expatiates on the themes of the greatness both of human sin and of God's remedy for it. But now the paradox appears: the Apostle conflicts with the believer. As believer, Paul is a wretched sinner wholly dependent upon the undeserved miracle of divine grace and forgiveness, and committed therefore to a devotedly submissive feminine ethic of grateful love and dedicated service. But as an Apostle, Paul is committed to an entirely different ethic and character-type. He needs to be an

authoritarian jealous father-figure, and indeed in the early
Christian iconography the Apostle/Bishop was commonly regarded as an icon of God, rather than of Christ.

As Apostle Paul is an insecure and jealous father, as believer he
must be a joyfully meek and devoted wife. Being Paul, he finds it
rather a strain to be both of these characters at once in the same
text. But that is not all, for Paul has a second conflict to deal with
too. Thus far we have spoken of Christianity only as a religion of
domination and submission, a power-religion. It has another
aspect, of which Paul is also aware and which is at variance with
his other pre-occupations. For the earliest Christianity is also, in a
veiled and implicit way, a religion of human liberation. It hints,
and Paul hints, that God has given himself to human beings
through his Son and in his Spirit so completely and so irrevocably
that the whole power-submission trip is over. God once was
personified absolute Power, physical, moral and spiritual power.
Even today we can in certain Muslim lands still sense that terrible
Power brooding over people. Yet the Christian message is that the
stupendous old cosmic disjunction (high-low, power-weakness,
holiness-sin) is now ended. The Power has liquidated itself by
passing into those over whom it was formerly exercised. Just the
fact of Christ-and-the-Spirit is the death of God. The Law is now
written in our hearts and the Power over us has become a power
within us. God has redeemed us by dying for us. Now he lives on
in our hearts and we are identified with him. The old conflict is
over and alienation is at an end. We can give up that obsessive
concern with giving and getting *permission* from above all the
time. In one strand of his text, Paul recognizes that human beings
are now liberated. Domination and hierarchy are outdated
because the godman means the end of the gulf between God and
man. Vaguely Paul knows this, but he cannot follow it through.
He is still too hooked on the erotic excitements of power and
weakness, holiness and sin, domination and tearfully-grateful
submission. And the reason *why* he is hooked is that the split
between the wielder of power and its victim is a split within his
own psychology.[6] By that in turn I mean a split within his texts.
But we have been reading his texts ever since he wrote them, not
to mention the fact that many or most of the other New
Testament texts manifest at least something of the same split. So
the old Western Christian self has not been transmitted through

all these centuries by any occult means. It has been created by Paul's text, as in each generation he has become interwoven with us.

Nor is the influence confined to the realm of psychology. The tensions that animate Paul's text also reveal themselves on the large scale in church history, where the institutional power-religion with its characteristic form of selfhood has always been in conflict with another and more wayward charismatic faith and form of selfhood. Paul is so early, and his institutional status as an Apostle and prince of the church is so open to question, that he can be seen about equally plausibly as a charismatic and as an institutional leader, and the two different personality-types can both look back to him.

The long-standing religious conflict that grows out of Paul's text can be summarized thus:

Institution	Charisma
The Church	The Spirit
Doctrine	Mysticism
Order	Freedom
Law	Gospel
Obedience	Expression
Hierarchy	Equality
An objective, public authority-system	The authority-principle internalized

Since the Enlightenment we have always tended to misunderstand this conflict. We think, in Voltairean style, of a mighty obscurantist institution (left-hand column) being challenged by the free rational individual (right-hand column). That is mistaken, because subjective or privatized rationalism began only with Descartes. In classical and medieval times, right up to the Enlightenment, Reason was out there. It was objective, expressed in cosmic logos and cosmic law and manifest in a public order of things that rightly demanded the individual's loyalty and obedience. You became a rational individual not in opposition to but by participation in and conformity to this great cosmic and institutional order.

So what I am calling old Western selfhood belongs entirely on the left side of the line. In literature it is best exemplified by Paul, Tertullian, Augustine, Luther, Calvin, Pascal and Kierkegaard.

The structure of the self is expressed in the theology these writers produced, and it is a Master-Slave structure. Passionate believers, they have internalized a super-extreme polarity between a God who just couldn't be more Holy, Mighty, Infinite and near in Judgment, and a human being who just couldn't be more wretched, abject and contemptible. Complicated dialectics are introduced to resolve the polarity but inevitably they also entrench it.

Internalized, the Holy God/sinful man, Master/slave, not-my-will-but-thine psychology has very striking effects. It makes for an inner life which is highly self-conscious because I have internalized God's view of me as well as having my own view of me, and also highly dramatic because the oppositions within the self are so extreme. Furthermore, the Master/slave psychology gives me standards to live by. It is a kind of enhanced platonism in that respect, and everyone who has been brought up within the Master/slave psychology has a very deep fear of giving it up. I know the Master/slave structure makes me feel guilty all the time, but at least if I feel guilty then I do have standards, whereas if I gave up the Master/slave psychology and lost my guilt I'd feel nothing. I would just fall into nihilism and *anomie*. That's the fear: dim twentieth-century people attack Christianity for making people chronically guilty, but it's a sight better to have a God in you who makes you feel guilty than to be unable to feel anything at all. If I feel guilty then at least I still have some indirect and faint notion of what the innocent and the Holy might be, whereas if I don't I haven't.

The case is a strong one. For twenty years I continued to read Kierkegaard. I thought: this old Western self is tragic, divided and afflicted, but at least it's *something*, and it's better to be something than to be nothing. So people locked into the old Western Master/slave psychology will be unwilling to abandon it until they are persuaded that there is some way of getting as much value at a lower psychic cost.

Alternatively we may be able to argue ourselves out of old-Western selfhood if we can carry through a critical reduction of it. That will involve showing that this form of selfhood is not 'natural' – a fitting response to cosmic facts – but was an artefact, created by power to be power's tool.

Consider this: standard Western theology once said that human beings in their natural state are so offensive to God that new-born babes, as yet unbaptized, deserve his damnation. Furthermore

God has the longest possible memory, for every least little thing you ever did to offend him is going to be brought up in evidence against you on Judgment Day. Now apologists have often pointed out that these fearsome doctrines, and others like them, imply a very high view of the self. What we are and what we do matters a lot to God and never gets to matter any less. The self is continuant, self-identical, substantial, and morally-responsible without any statute of limitations.

Fine, but all this is not as good as it looks. In fact it's even *worse* than it looks. The doctrine makes me acutely aware of my predicament as one who is forever, eternally, stuck with undiminishing plenary responsibility for every least misdeed and faced with the certainty of punishment. We can begin to see just how terroristic the ideas are if we grasp that God's detection rate is 100%, that his wrath is as terrible as can be, and that in relation to him the sinner is a torture victim deprived of the hope of release by death.

There is a remedy: the doctrine of redemption leads me through a psychodrama, standard for all believers and described in standard language, through which I can get justification and a straight walk to final salvation. However, the redemption drama leaves me utterly dependent upon Grace and wholly committed to the church's teachings and practices. So the extent to which I am freed is limited; in some ways I am made more dependent than ever. That indeed was the object of the exercise.

Thus the old-Western-Christian (*i*) conception of reason as objective and cosmic; (*ii*) conception of the self as an immortal, substantial, free and morally accountable rational agent; and (*iii*) standard psychodrama of redemption – were all three of them intimately interlinked. Certainly there was in the West a strong tradition of individualism and vivid self-awareness, but what actually made the Westerner so self-conscious was the probing and thorough religious terrorism to which she was subjected. Thus, far from being set against the public and institutional, the old Western self was entirely its product, having been created by power for power to be power's reliable tool.

The Western self trembles with the violence of the great forces that have produced it. Are we to say that the theology is so fierce because the church was faced with the task of civilizing a miscellany of violent tribespeople in a turbulent corner of the world, or are we to say that Europe's history is drenched in blood because we have professed the cruellest of all theologies? Who can tell? – but I dare to suggest that what finally killed off the old theology was not so much the Enlightenment or any purely intellectual change, but just Napoleon. With the end of the *ancien régime* and the rise of the modern bourgeois state in Europe came enormous technical improvements in social administration. It was this more than any other single factor that eventually persuaded Europeans that an acceptable degree of social order could be maintained without the old system of religious terrorism. In Britain, for example, many people in the Establishment continued to hold that 'the religious sanction' (i.e., the fear of Hell) was necessary until about 1860, after which Hell steadily faded and God became more kindly.[7] Reason has since become less cosmic-law, more internalized, human and plural. The self, no longer so inflamed with guilt and fear, has become resolved down into the flux of history and culture. It is cooler, less enduring, takes itself less seriously and is readier now to acknowledge its own transience and secondariness.

Paradoxically, the self is now therefore able to be more ethically active. The old Western self was, ethically speaking, terrorized into impotence like a rabbit by a stoat. In a sadomasochistic relationship the dominant partner insists that the other may not make the slightest move without permission. The relation between God and the soul used to be like that, for it was erotic and was characterized by extreme inequality of power between the partners. Notoriously, the psychology involved here is addictive and hard to get out of. When we leave such a relationship there is doubtless metaphysical loss, but it is offset by the ethical gain. In the older world-view what made you important and gave worth to your life was your immortal soul, your eternal moral responsibility, the cosmic grandeur of the myth that held you fast, and the weight of your religious duties and your destiny. In the newer world-view what makes you important and gives worth to your life is your creativity, your capacity to become a self not quite like any other and your capacity to communicate yourself in a unique way in your relations with others. You're not immortal; you are only a part of the flux. But the flux matters because of what everybody puts into it, and you have your own contribution to make. You must therefore claim your human rights, as must each and all of us.

The new Christian self that comes forward to replace the old Western self is therefore merely secondary, communicative and social. There is no real, essential me. I'm just an intersection in the human network. I am communication all through. My ethic therefore will affirm communication, self-giving, self-loss, expression, creativity and the production of ever-new metaphors, meanings and life-styles. The Christianized version of our modern reality will thus aim to be a bit more generous and selfless than the rather tight secular ethic of fighting for one's human rights. It will be supererogatory, seeing life as a holy communion.

But we have some way to go yet in our attempt to show that it is as good as the old Western selfhood that we have lost.

(d) Mysticism and Socialism

One way of finding out what people believe about the self is to examine their ideas about the ultimate goal of human life. This was regularly the subject of a formal treatise in the older books of theology. It was called the *tractatus de fine ultimo* and dealt with beatitude, Heaven and the Vision of God. These were by no means recondite topics. The ways of thinking involved pervaded the culture. Classical thought was often individualistic and in the heyday of ancient philosophy, which was also the period when the great religions were taking shape, it was customary to present your teaching as a spiritual discipline and an ethical path for the individual which if followed assiduously would lead to perfect blessedness of soul. Furthermore, the biblical ideas of linear time and of God's guidance of all worldly events towards a final consummation had some parallels in Greek thought. A theory of Providence can be found in Plato, and Aristotle was a highly teleological thinker who saw each and every thing in nature as gravitating towards a pre-set and inbuilt goal. Everything had been made for a purpose. So the medieval treatise on Man's Last End was only one manifestation of the generally 'finalistic' or teleological character of Western thought. In the nineteenth century Hegel, the Catholic Church, Karl Marx and liberal protestants such as Tennyson were unanimous in their belief in 'one far-off divine event / To which the whole creation moves'. We can go further: to this day people's notion of the meaning of life is finalistic. That is, people still think that the world in general and our life in particular are meaningful insofar as all events in them subserve a single overarching, unfolding cosmic Purpose which is drawing all things towards a blessed completion. Life is meaningful if it has a destination, if we are getting somewhere, if the future is going to be better than the past and if, ultimately, everything that is good is going to be conserved.

Since Aristotle and the Old Testament prophets, then, nearly all of Western thought has been finalistic. Confidence in this area has broken down only in the past hundred years.

Yet alongside the vast importance of finalistic thinking for over twenty-three centuries we have to set its rather baffling vagueness. There has got to be an attainable blessed future state to make life meaningful – or so people think; but the accounts of it are extremely diverse, and individually very unclear. Is it an embodied state or a disembodied, is it mystical or is it social, is it a future condition of this earth or are we to think of another world? There is no one agreed picture; instead we are presented with a range of myths. It is an example of the general principle that what is important in a culture is not that some particular doctrine is well-understood and widely held, but rather that the culture's characteristic value-conflicts give to the whole field of discourse a distinctive shape. But that generalization needs to be explained in a little more detail.

Western thought about the goal of human life moves on a field which has six dimensions or axes.

The *first* is the *knowledge-love* axis. At one extreme, blessedness is a state of absolute knowledge. It is the complete soul-satisfaction I have when I am in a state of timeless, pure rational intuition of absolute necessity of being. It is so, it must be so, I see that it is so and I see why it must be so, and there is no further question or cause for dissatisfaction. Such is the ultimate goal of the theoretical or contemplative life, but as just described it is a completely asocial ideal and might even be considered amoral. So at the opposite extreme we may place those visions of the highest good which give the first place to 'pure personal relations' or to the spiritual marriage. Love counts for more than knowledge. In the most thoroughgoing accounts the blessed state is seen as an ecstatic self-surrender into pure Love, in which knowledge and even consciousness have been renounced.

The *second* axis could be called *instant-journey*. In Western (as also in Buddhist) thought there is a contrast between those who believe that the blessed state can be attained more or less instantaneously by conversion, by baptism, by spiritual rebirth, by a sudden illumination of the mind or by an abrupt and revolutionary transformation of consciousness; and on the other hand those who see the blessed state as the goal of a long pilgrimage, discipline or ascent that may take lifetimes to complete.

Thirdly there is the *natural-supernatural* axis. Some follow Aristotle in being chiefly (or Marx in being exclusively) interested in whatever sort of personal fulfilment may be immanently realizable – that is, attainable by us here and now in this body and in this life. This tradition of thought is of long standing; a naturalistic and this-worldly vein entered Catholicism in the thirteenth century and flowered in the Italian Renaissance. But of course there has always been in parallel with it a line of teaching and preaching which says that, on the contrary, any natural End or fulfilment that we may seek to attain is infinitely surpassed in importance by our supernatural End, eternal happiness in the Vision of God.

This leads us at once to the *fourth*, *subjective-objective* axis. An old Greek tradition implies that to be really happy you have to be a substance, a distinct, independent, active and self-sufficient being. In which case we will be inclined to portray eternal happiness as a state of the self, beatitude. However, there is a contrary and biblical tradition which says that the happiest life is the life of someone who is not self-sufficient but is completely given over and dedicated to the service of a supremely good and perfect Lord. For such a person the supreme good is not a state of oneself but, quite simply, the Glory of God. There are many marxists and Christians who would agree with Freud in saying that the old monastic ideal – *solitudo*, *beatitudo* – misses the mark. The highest good for us is that we should have a dedicated, active and social life: 'love and work'.

We begin to see interconnections among the axes, for the *fifth* that we have to describe is the *individual-social* axis. The blessed state may be pictured as a perfect society, the Kingdom of God, the City of God, the new Jerusalem or the communist society, or it may be portrayed as the flight of the alone to the Alone, the individual's mystical union with God.

Finally there is the *resurrection-immortality* axis. If the blessed state has to be a state of the whole person, then we will prefer to speak of the resurrection of the body. A recent study has indicated that with the decline of the old monastic ideal and the development of a higher Christian valuation of sexual love, there has in the past two centuries or so been much talk not just about bodiliness but also about sexual life after death. Others, however, stand in a more Hellenistic tradition that is apt to regard the body as an encumbrance. They think Charles Kingsley's drawings of bonking in Heaven[8] risible, and they prefer to speak of the immortality of the soul.

In a moment I will attempt a reduction of these six axes to one, but for the present let us say that they define the field over which Western writers moved in their discussions about the telos or goal of human life. More than that, the six axes define the most important *value-polarities* in Western culture. I also suggest that in many ways we would see ethical questions more clearly if we were to give up talking of just simple, single values, and were instead *to treat the atomic moral object as a value-polarity*.

The tradition, I am suggesting, never presents us with a value that stands singly but always with values that are scaled, differential and in dialectical relation, in tension or in conflict. Thus, the mainline philosophical tradition doubtless regards theoretical knowledge as the most important thing of all for us human beings, whereas the ecstatic, radical, christocentric strain in Christianity puts love first. From this polarity spring the traditional oppositions of Greece and the Bible, theory and practice, contemplative and active, understanding the world and changing the world. But the oppositions are complicated by the fact that there is also an eros-strand in platonism, and a vigorous contemplative-monastic tradition in Christianity. This means that knowledge and love, contemplative and active and so forth get to be in a very intricate, Hegelian sort of dialectical relationship with each other in our tradition. And perhaps no great cultural system presents a straightforward and tidy system of values. Rather, it presents us with the complex set of value-conflicts and tensions that energize it and give to it its distinctive flavour.

There is a well-known principle in science that the best theory is not the one that finally and unambiguously states the truth and shuts everyone up. What would be the point of such a theory; who *wants* final truth? Final truth is death. No, the best theory is the one that sparks off the greatest amount of *further* controversy, research and speculation. The best theory is the most productive. Analogously, we can try to get our ingrained platonism out of our heads and say that perhaps the best moral tradition is the one that is so packed with stimulating, tightly-sprung tensions, conflicts and dialectical oppositions that it prompts the most subsequent moral striving. A moral tradition has to be dynamic. It has to *activate* people to moral endeavour, and to do this it needs to be full of spiritual polarities. The more searching they are and the more they bite into our souls, the better for us. Thus the Enlightenment attempt to systematize morality was utterly misguided, for a *system* of *morality* is a contradiction in terms. Morality is powered by value-conflict, and where there is no longer any serious value-conflict there is no longer any morality either. From Greek tragedy onwards the moral situation was typically the moral *dilemma*, the state of moral conflict.

This, then, is perhaps why neither in Christianity nor in the other main sub-traditions of Western culture do we find any very clear portrayal in descriptive terms of exactly what we may expect to find when we reach the goal of our life. It isn't in fact possible that there should be 'literally true' belief by Christians in life after death, by marxists in the communist society, or by platonists in immortal life in the noumenal realm. Necessarily, because the culture gives us only a lot of value-tensions that goad us into choosing and aiming and striving, there cannot be just one true description of the *telos* as a forthcoming state of affairs. Necessarily, any particular account of the *telos* is just an art-vision. A creative person or group has a perspective upon the received traditional set of value-polarities, and seeks to resolve them artistically into an organic unity. The number of such possible art-visions is indefinitely large, but none of them is or can be a Michelin guide. An eschatological vision is not that kind of thing.

Pictures of our human destiny, then, are not to be taken for forecasts. Their factual content is minimal. In any case the old finalistic ways of thinking have broken down.

However, there remains the possibility of a path to beatitude that does not presuppose any finalistic beliefs. One might see the peak of life as lying in some non-metaphysical, and indeed non-cognitive, mystical experience or state of soul. It may just be the case that some highly blissful psychological state *happens* to be attainable by the use of certain techniques that somebody *happens* to have discovered. None of this need have been supernaturally predestined. The state of bliss was perhaps not preplanned, the way to it was not supernaturally revealed to us and it need not be supposed that we are being guided like trams on rails towards Heaven. The *summum bonum* might be simply an available option, something we can try for as we may try for proficiency at sport.

Theories of this type – non-metaphysical, non-supernaturalist accounts of beatitude – are popular for obvious reasons. It would indeed be wonderful if we could get to the goal of the religious life without having to believe any lies or nonsense. There are three paths on offer.

1. *Unlearn the way down to where you already are!* Krishnamurti, Alan Watts and a number of other Eastern-influenced teachers appear to hold that beatitude is a state of pure unconditioned awareness. At a deep transcendental level we are always already in it, but normally it is hidden from us by layers and layers of false consciousness. Language, conceptual thought and all the products of our own desires and anxieties have drastically blinkered our vision. So the way to blessedness is by an unlearning that makes us more and more open and free. We must simply *doff* all authorities, group-allegiances, creeds, words and so on. Truth is a pathless land, so that paradoxically the way to it is by forgetting all the marked footpaths. We have to unlearn our way down to beatitude.[9]

Krishnamurti's message is fascinating in its religious radicalism, and for his own attempt to put it consistently into practice. But it is of course meaningless. One way of making the point is to say that interpretation goes all the way down. There cannot be an awareness that is not already conditioning its own content. Alternatively we can make the point by saying that Krishnamurti is using language to recommend to us a state of consciousness that is allegedly wholly outside language. But this ineffable, *ex hypothesi*, cannot within the symbolism of language be given any content, nor is there any way of pointing in its direction. So as Krishnamurti himself says, he isn't saying anything and *cannot* be saying anything. He can only say why there is nothing that can be said.

That by no means disposes of Krishnamurti, and I shall return to him shortly. Meanwhile the other purportedly non-finalistic ways to beatitude can be mentioned more briefly.

2. *Obey, school, drill yourself for years and years, and you will become a saint!* We are thinking here of the traditional ascetic pathway of the Christian, Buddhist or Hindu holy man. It could be that as a learned and practised discipline the way to holiness might indeed make saints of us, independently of the truth or otherwise of any particular metaphysical beliefs. Unfortunately, agreed and reliable *public* criteria of the success of a spiritual discipline are lacking. In their absence we have no more to go on than what the holy say for themselves, and our own impression of their behaviour. The evidence is inconclusive. Some holy people seem to go soft in the head and others to become bigots. We have all met people, especially certain very young ones, who seem to be just naturally good by accident. They have had no special training at all, but we cannot think of any way of improving upon them. I do not know how to give the concept of sainthood any further assessible content beyond that.

3. *Hilarity and mania.* Some writers just identify the goal of the religious life with an abnormal state of consciousness. It is described as a condition of ecstatic joy and super-real perception of the world, a 'peak-experience'. It is usually very transient, but it can be artificially induced by drugs.

Since on my own showing we are the conferrers of value, so that something is valuable if we choose to make it so, I cannot demonstrate to a drug- or peak-experience-addict that his personal decision to assign supreme value to certain psychological states is irrational and should be given up. He must do as he wishes. But I can of course say to him that by retreating into a private and ineffable realm he cuts himself off from the rest of humanity. The price for having taken up a position that is beyond criticism is that he cannot satisfactorily explain or defend himself in the public language. Necessarily, ineffable truth is a bankrupt idea; you pay so much for it that you can do nothing with it. And the same is true of contentless but supremely blissful states of soul: if I cannot say to your satisfaction just what the soul-state *is*, *why* it makes me so happy and *why* I judge it to be so valuable – then I must expect to be disregarded, for I have not provided your understanding with anything that it can chew on.

Until recently it was difficult to say more about the issue than that. Kantians, empiricists and others joined in declaring that claims to have had very important but ineffable religious experiences and sudden flashes of insight into ultimate truth have got to be disregarded. If they don't have a content that can be spelled out in the common language and subjected to some kind of public scrutiny and assessment, then necessarily we can do nothing with them, they can mean nothing to us and there's nothing for us *but* to disregard them. Each day letters to me arrive from worthy folk who have found in a flash the ineffable secret of the universe and the meaning of life. It all seems very important to them, and they want to make me say that it seems equally important to me. But in terms of the traditional mainline philosophy I have to say, 'What makes it seem so important to you is the fact that it came in a flash to you; but the fact that it came in a flash to you is precisely the reason why *I* have no option but to disregard it. What makes it mean such a lot to you is just what makes it mean nothing at all to me. For, necessarily, the only common meaning is linguistic meaning. *Experience does not exist*; can you understand that? Only the public is real, and experience is not public. Your supposed experience may seem meaningful to you, but only your *words* can mean anything to me. Only language is common and public. Experience is not.'

As I have said, until about a generation ago that was about as far as the argument could be taken. There can be no doubt about the continuing importance of the issue. It underlies the whole of the Western debate about our Last End, for, as we hinted, the six axes which define the field all in the end come down to one. Do we say that the highest good for us human beings has got to be social, bodily, communicative and linguistic; or do we look for some transcendent, spiritual, intuitive state of solitary mystic bliss? Do we believe in the City of God or in the Vision of God? The social view of human beings says that our whole reality as persons is social and communicative. We are not substances; we consist in our external relations, that is, in what we are to each other. Subjectivity is secondary, a kind of by-product. By contrast, the mystical view of human beings says that there is something in us which transcends our social relations. We are immortal souls, substances that will endure.

Thus Krishnamurti's talk of pure unconditional awareness, the saint's talk of the vision of God, Aldous Huxley's rhapsodies about mescalin, and my more eccentric correspondents' claims to have experienced in a flash the meaning of life – these and many more like them are in their varied and picturesque ways all variants upon the same basic claim. A human being, it is alleged, is not just made of language, differences, fleeting social relations and secondariness. There is something in us that reaches to the very bottom of things, that is substantial and that transcends secondariness and contingency. We are capable of an intuitive and infallible apprehension of what is primary. In the end, human beings can get up to the top floor and meet the guy who runs the whole show. We can be let in on the secret. We are capable of absolute knowledge.

That is the claim. Plato endorses it, so that versions of it run through the history of Western philosophy. Religious forms of it are found almost everywhere. It explains why my correspondents think it perfectly sensible for them to claim that they, ordinary folk, without any special talents, qualifications or effort on their part, should have suddenly heard from the Boss the secret of the Universe.

The claim has been able to persist for so long because Western philosophy has so persistently sought transcendence. Plato's doctrine of absolute knowledge held, broadly, until the Enlightenment and has since been revived in new forms by Spinoza, Hegel and others. More generally, figures like Descartes gave a fresh lease of life to the idea that we can have immediate and certain knowledge of at least some things that are foundational and primary. The two really important examples that Descartes cites are our own existence as spiritual subjects, and sense-experience. Descartes created our popular scientific realism by his conviction that interpretation does *not* reach all the way down. We can separate out an uninterpreted and sheerly-given sense-datum. Infallible, absolute knowledge of a pure given is possible. At the instant in which a sense-experience first enters into our sensibility we cannot be wrong about it, as also we cannot be wrong about ourselves. Only when we begin to interpret does the possibility of error arise. Before that point the sense-datum is the pure object of our absolute knowledge, like God for the blessed in Heaven. The visual datum is like the Vision of God. I can't be wrong about it and me and its presentation to me.

No doubt science would not have been able to displace theology unless Descartes had managed to entrench this extraordinary doctrine in our culture. As it is, it passed into British empiricism and into scientific folklore, and became part of the more general pattern in Western thought that distinguishes between what is primarily given to us and what we secondarily build upon it. As we distinguish between observation and inference, so we also distinguish between fact and interpretation, base and super-structure. This pattern gives the believer in religious experience some leverage, for it permits her to go on thinking that, whether or not she's interpreted it correctly, there is still something *there* which is just given. Thus we may still find today that a vague theological realism, a vague conviction that we are immortal souls and a vague belief in life after death and seeing the face of God all persist, even after people have largely abandoned the standard theological articulation of these ideas. Realism staggers on because of the belief in the pure and primary datum, an objective pre-linguistic Given that is better than and prior to our inadequate interpretations of it. They may fail, but it stands.

Not any more. Cartesianism has broken down, empiricism has broken down and the belief in a pure given has broken down, chiefly perhaps because of what has happened in recent French philosophy.

British philosophy after Descartes was planned by John Locke to be the herald and handmaid of natural science. Our sensibility was an empty receptacle. Data swam into it and presented themselves already coloured, shaped, determinate and smartly turned-out. The human observer combined them, generalized about them and theorized about them, his pronouncements being always subject to verification by checking them against the incoming stream of further ready-made data.

This was a philosophy invented to function as an ideological justification for the new natural science. The two key doctrines, that the mind is a blank slate and that incoming data arrive already determinate and intelligible, were designed to persuade us of the objectivity and reliability of our empirical knowledge.

They do more than that. They also say, 'The emptier your head and the more you make a completely fresh start, the more solid and objective will be the empirical knowledge you build'. So Locke's teachings are subversive. He is quietly telling us to forget tradition, culture and the social training of the mind. They do not help. Instead Locke teaches a lesson which the English have taken gratefully to heart: the most reliable chap is the most perfect philistine. Trust the evidence of your own senses and your own feelings. In them and nowhere else is truth.

Now the lines along which this doctrine may be criticized are familiar. Kant proved that the mind is not a blank slate. No knowledge is possible unless the understanding very thoroughly processes the raw material presented to it. So there is in our heads a lot of processing machinery. It is the same in each of us who reads English as her native language, but it cannot quite be *a priori* in the strong sense as Kant claimed, for during the nineteenth century people became aware that the way we think and see the world is (like language itself) shaped by culture and subject to historical change. But what *is* historical change? Conceptions of what it is and whether it is getting anywhere are *themselves* also subject to historical change. That destroys Objectivity and Truth, for now it is clear that we don't have to think the way we do; our culture just happens to have evolved making us think the way we do. Indeed the way we think *works*, but then, many other ways of thinking also work.

Thus far we have reached the point that Nietzsche had already reached in the 1870s. It implies a reversal, a turning upside down of previous ways of thinking. If culture determines the way we think, then the secondary after all comes first. Superstructures must be put before base, theory before observation, interpretation before fact and (inevitably) Society before the Individual and Culture before Nature.

Something of all this has already become widely diffused in Anglo-Saxon thought, but it has been taken very much further in France. French philosophy is based on the human sciences rather than on the natural sciences, and in the human sciences it is obvious that the background system or structure must precede the individual occurrence.[10]

Suppose we set out to study the game of chess by the methods of natural science and British empiricism. We study actual moves made, theorize about them – and we get nowhere. You cannot understand what is the point of a particular move in chess except against the background of a *prior* understanding of what a game is, what is the object of the game of chess, what are the rules of chess, and why the player selected this particular move out of the range of possible moves that was available. We cannot judge whether she made a good move except by reference to all that she could have done but chose not to do. Without that holistic background understanding of the game in your head, you cannot know what's going on.

As with chess, so with language. Saussure used the word *langue* for the whole system that must be presupposed before particular utterances can either be generated or understood. Somehow, society trains a knowledge of the *langue* into each of us with remarkable uniformity. This collective and social background precedes and makes possible the individual performance. Saussure's contemporary Durkheim rather similarly showed how society shapes the way we see the world by training us in a large stock of 'collective representations'. Again the message is that the cultural superstructure precedes the individual. It comes first, and it both shapes perception and makes possible our personal performances. It pre-determines what sort of data can enter and in what form they must present themselves.

Without going into excessive detail, let us sum up. The empiricist saw the mind as a *camera obscura* in which the world is reflected just as it is. The sense-datum arrives already coloured, shaped, intelligible and informative. I apprehend the thing-in-itself, just as it is. But the newer structuralist outlook sees our sensibility as highly pre-programmed by culture. It is like a pin-ball machine in an amusement arcade: when it is poked in some particular area there is a ping and a flash – and *that* is what experience is.

For the empiricist, if I see yellow it is because something yellow has just come in. For the structuralist, if I see yellow it is because a particular area in my sensibility (not orange, not green, but *yellow*) has just fired.

Now mark the difference: the empiricist's mind is blank, and experience enters ready-formed. So *form precedes language*. There is thus no reason *a priori* why one day she may not have an experience quite novel in form and for which she has no words. Nothing strictly precludes the possibility of such an experience. So empiricism is and must be receptive to supernatural, religious, ineffable mystical experiences. But the structuralist is in a very different position. My sensibility has been trained and differentiated by culture. An experience is just a firing in one particular differentiated zone. I cannot experience a thing unless I have been pre-programmed by culture to be capable of experiencing it. If some particular differentiation within my sensibility has never been established it cannot fire. If a meaning is not already imprinted upon my constitution, it cannot become excited. There is no experience which is not the firing of a meaning, and therefore, if the structuralist account of the matter is to be accepted (as indeed it clearly must be) all mystical ideas about extraordinary experiences about the ineffable and about pure unconditioned awareness are dead.

Of course mystical ideas may *themselves* be part of the imprinted culture. But in that case they themselves have a purely natural history, like our other concepts. People don't care to hear that. It's hard to grasp. But ideas about transcendence are in themselves . . . just immanent; supernatural beliefs are just . . . natural phenomena; mystical experiences of stepping right out of time . . . have a natural history *in* time. If someone comes along in great excitement and tells us that last night God appeared to him and told him that soon the world will come to an end, then we can reply, Yes, and this experience of yours has *itself* a three-thousand-year history, starting with Amos perhaps, a history that fully explains why your experience took the form it did.

Thus the structuralist – and still more, the post-structuralist – point of view finally seals the death of God, if by 'God' we mean supernaturalism and the sort of mysticism that fancies it can usefully seek to escape from ordinary consciousness and ordinary language. That sort of mysticism and that sort of God are utterly finished. The self's whole life is lived inside ordinary language, ordinary consciousness and history. There is no outside. The conclusion therefore is that we must decisively choose socialism and reject mysticism. That is, the highest good for us human beings has got to be social, bodily, communicative and linguistic. There is not and there cannot be anything else for us. We must accept the non-substantial, the radically social, the external-relations and therefore the *ethical* view of the self. We have to break with the long Western tradition of supposing that only a substantial self is a fully morally-responsible self. The opposite is the case; instead of the old pseudo-ethic of purifying our own immortal souls and preparing them for the next life, we need a new and more Christian ethic of pouring ourselves out like Christ into the common life of humanity.

(e) Prayer and Creativity

The proposition that we do not have immortal souls is just as mythical as the proposition that we do have them. Less misleadingly, we should say that we now need to abandon the old Augustine-and-Descartes habit of starting with the mind and the inner life. Human beings cannot think except in signs. Powers of the soul such as rationality cannot be exercised except in sentence-structures. Thought presupposes language. But nobody can invent her own first language; language, and *therefore* 'the mind' and 'thought' and the rest of it, is society's gift to us. So human reality is primarily outward, interactive and communicational. It is only secondarily, and as a kind of specialized by-product, inward, mental and soulish. For example, it is only after we have been taught to do sums outwardly on paper that we can subsequently learn a shorthand version of this activity and do mental arithmetic.

The change of viewpoint called for is typically twentieth-century, but surprisingly difficult to carry through consistently. The pull of the old logic and metaphysics remains very strong. For when we reverse the order and declare that the outward and bodily is prior to the inward and mental, we are not only saying that society precedes the individual and that language constitutes the self. We are also saying quite generally that relations are prior to substances. This doctrine is implied by Saussure's dictum that 'there are no positive terms in language', because the whole system of *langue* is just a system of differences. Meaning is always differential and relative, and meaning comes first. For particular concrete utterances always presuppose *langue*, and *langue* is a general system of relativities which as yet includes no proper names nor any reference to concrete objects. So sense is prior to reference and, in metaphysics, relations come before things. And that is a very difficult idea to grasp.

In religion it means that we have to give up the old Augustinian idea that the real me is the me at private prayer. My reality is first and foremost relational and linguistic. I am the sum of all my communicative interactions with other people. That being so, I can just about see how public prayer makes sense – or at least, might make sense. In expressive and symbolic ritual action and language, public prayer binds the community together in mutual support and in the affirmation of common values. In times of communal disaster and at moments of transition in life, even the most secular people in the most secularized societies still instinctively gather in the ancient way. Private prayer is more puzzling but may perhaps be viewed as a secondary derivative of and substitute for public prayer, an internalized ritual like the 'spiritual communion' sometimes practised by Catholics.

That, however, does not dispose of all the problems of prayer. The God of public prayer is an embodiment of communal values. The ritual behaviour and the vocabulary that we use in approaching him are borrowed from occasions such as an absolute Monarch's regular audience or a feudal homage ceremony. But feudalism and absolute monarchy have vanished from our secular life, leaving us feeling embarrassed and foolish at having to abase ourselves in such extravagant language when we are in church. It is only after tragic and violent deaths that our sense of our own weakness and wickedness becomes for a while strong enough for us to be able to use church language without discomfort.

There is a second problem, in that the received forms of worship make little allowance for human creativity. Rite and ceremony, text and ritual action are canonized or prescribed by tradition. There is almost no scope for individuals to make a personal contribution.

Forms of worship do exist which meet these difficulties. Quaker worship is not so courtly, objectifying and obsessed with power, and individuals are encouraged to contribute something of their own. Secondly, *all* scriptural religions are in a sense religions of the death of the gods. They all say that the age of prophecy is past. God has withdrawn to Heaven and is no longer around with quite the old immediacy, but he has left us the Book as a souvenir. Thus in all scriptural religions the recitation and study of scripture becomes itself a recognized form of worship, quiet, reflective and allowing for some exercise of human creativity in meditating upon and interpreting the text.

Mainline Western churches are still basilicas, fourth-century royal audience-halls constructed for the cult of the Emperor. No doubt in the future the place of public worship will have to borrow more from the Jewish study-house and the Quaker Meeting-Room.

The problem of how to do it with conviction is nowadays especially acute in the case of private prayer. Just as we no longer deliberate by soliloquizing out loud, so we no longer need to pray to an objective God in order to get a critical perspective upon ourselves. In both cases we are highly embarrassed at being found still to need such an old-fashioned device.

The history is distinctly ironical. Traditionally, when I prayed I addressed a God out there over against me. He was the embodiment of everything that I was committed to and judged myself by. He was my values, my superego, my ego-ideal, my reference-point, my Lord. He kept me up to the mark and made me conscious of myself. I developed myself through the drama of my relation to him. He was a real, a natural and a necessary personification. However, in the seventeenth century the modern Individual Self was formed in North-West Europe. It was added on to the human world because it was going to be needed by the new bourgeois culture. An ethic of individualism was developing along with the market economy. Even in modest private houses, people were getting separate bedrooms. Life was becoming privatized and so was faith. At the time it was supposed that the new subjective consciousness would be beneficial to Christian faith, making private prayer in particular more vivid and emotional and impressing upon all alike the importance of personal conversion and holiness of life.

At first everything went as expected. Pietism and Methodism flourished. But the new bourgeois subjectivity, which at first enhanced personal piety, by the nineteenth century was making an objective God redundant. It all came to a crisis in Kierkegaard. Nobody could have been more passionately committed to bourgeois subjectivity and personal religion. But in his first, aesthetic, literature we see him steadily working his way out of theological realism. In the second and more specifically Christian literature of his later years, Kierkegaard is painfully divided. He has turned to Christian ethics and has read and admired Feuerbach. At times he seems to be given over to the love of his neighbour and to have become a real Feuerbachian Christian, a whole human being. But at other times he still yearns for eternal happiness and a transcendent God to torment him.[11] To the true Feuerbachian Christian 'flesh-and-blood love' is 'the middle term' which reconciles the divine and the human. God is 'the realized Idea, the fulfilled law of morality, the moral nature of man posited as the absolute being', and the practice of love makes us whole by uniting us with our God. But poor Kierkegaard cannot quite accept reconciliation. He still longs for the old alienated theology that 'sets man's own nature before him as a separate nature, and moreover as a personal being who hates and curses sinners and excludes them from his grace, the only source of all salvation and happiness'.

In Kierkegaard private prayer to an objective God is gradually becoming spiritually pathological, and about half of him knows it. Bourgeois subjectivity by Kierkegaard's time had reached a point where it was perfectly capable of self-criticism without needing a transcendent God to look at it and judge it from outside. To try to keep the old theological objectivism going was to try to torment yourself by inwardly splitting yourself from your self – and why should a Christian need to do that to himself? In Kierkegaard the old belief in an objective transcendent God had become a refined technique of self-torture, as in effect he says in the last entries in his Journals.

It follows that a modern Christian must be very wary of private prayer, wary of the systematic self-deception, alienation and repression now involved in it. We may permit ourselves to use it only as a kind of imaginary participation in public worship which for some reason we cannot attend, or in a non-dualistic, reflective and expressive form. We may meditatively question ourselves, read quietly and think about our lives, our friends, our values. We may do these things if they help us with our real life, which is our life with others. But we must avoid like the plague any suggestion that our real life is the inner life.

What, though, of *freedom*? The modern social sciences, starting from Saussure and Durkheim, portray language and culture as a comprehensive social *a priori* within which we are held. Behind the individual utterance is the great socially-generated system of *langue*, behind the individual item of behaviour lies the whole social order. This vast structural background has brought us into being, for only by being raised in it have we emerged as subjects at all. We are subjects in our subjection to it. Only because it is there in the background can our particular performances and utterances be understood. I can't speak intelligibly except where *langue* is the common background matrix, and I cannot act unless the culture has already provided an interpretative context for my behaviour.

All this, however, does not threaten freedom so much as might at first appear, because explanation in the social sciences is structural rather than strictly deterministic. We understand a particular performance by reference to the background structure that has made its meaningfulness possible, by having prescribed in advance the range of possible forms of expression from among which this particular act has been selected. The explanation does not invoke antecedent efficient causes that (deterministically) *made* the action occur; instead, it fills in the background. A transcendental framework is presupposed, in the context of which the point of this action can be understood. If we may return to the chess analogy, the intelligibility of a particular move in chess depends upon a presupposed and common background understanding of what a game is, what the object of a game of chess is, what the powers of the pieces are and how by combinations of moves one can achieve the object of the game. I look at the move in the light of all the moves that might legally be made in this position, and try to work out what strong combinations are available to the player. If this move opens the strongest-available combination then it's the best move.

The chess commentator is able to explain the player's move by drawing upon his own background knowledge of chess. The situation is not strictly deterministic, for the player quite freely chooses which move to make. But he chooses one from among a finite range of options. And, in an important sense, the background structure has already anticipated every possible use that he can make of his freedom. It is the background structure that gives him the range of options and that makes one option rationally preferable and defensible. The rationality of a chess move, its intelligibility to others and their ability to evaluate it, all depend upon the background structure; and that structure must be held firm. An illegal move cannot be rational, cannot be understood and cannot be evaluated. It is an unthing, outside the game.

In religion we find a rather similar situation. At an early stage in its history every religion begins to drop into fixed forms of speech and practice. During the period of canonization there may be very sharp disputes about whether some particular form of words is to become a canonical expression or not. Consider in Christianity the phrases, 'the Son of God, born of the Virgin Mary, of one substance with the Father, God of God, God the Son, the God-bearer, the Mother of God'. Of these expressions only the first is scriptural. The canonization of the later ones took time and in some cases very fierce battles. But eventually things do become canonized, and thereafter the religious life is lived within a certain institutional order, a certain prescribed vocabulary and a certain range of permitted behaviours. There is some freedom; but it is relative to a structure which (under normal conditions, at least) is not open to change. A Christian who seeks to change the structure ceases to be a Christian, just as a chess player who insists on making an illegal move simply ceases to be playing chess. And to say this is not to be arbitrarily repressive; rather, the point is that freedom and intelligibility and evaluation are only *possible* against the background of an *a priori* social structure.

Now the question about human creativity can be formulated. There are two levels of freedom. There is the freedom of the orthodox, and there is the freedom of the transgressor. It is clear from our account that the freedom of the orthodox is real enough. The chess player can make a genuinely free and rational choice of the best from the available range of permitted moves, and can also innovate by discovering some theoretically interesting new line of play. So her freedom is real and there is no need to disparage it. However, if we are not to be sunk in what Nietzsche called 'Egyptianism', if we are to affirm the possibility of deep historical and cultural change, then there must also be such a thing as transgressive freedom and we need to give an account of it. This is not going to be easy, because transgressive freedom, by definition, is an incomprehensible unthing.

Nevertheless, we have to affirm it. Although Jesus appears not to have been a doctrinal heretic, he was indeed a moral and religious heretic who violated established frontiers and changed received valuations. Christianity is an essentially transgressive faith. 'Orthodox Christian' is an oxymoron, because the only true follower of Jesus is the heretic. Christianity must continually resist its own tendency to decay into an orthodoxy. Theologians today have to be rebels and dissidents. To be creative, Christian ethics must continually seek to subvert the established order and to change existing valuations. The faith is *about* justifying the ungodly, loving the unlovable, taking the side of the undeserving, reversing value-scales. For Christians, heresy is orthodoxy and transgression is obedience. The better you are the worse you are, and the worse you are the better you are.

So the question is, how is this possible? How does anybody ever get to be a religious rebel when by definition what he says and does is outrageous, impossible and incomprehensible? It transgresses its own possibility-conditions. Yet in some cases at least the rebel's work has been understood and has somehow become consolidated into the underlying structure as the basis of a new 'orthodoxy'.

It appears then that Christian ethics needs an account of how transgressive action is possible, and of how it can come to be understood and have lasting consequences.

The question would be utterly daunting if it were here arising for the first time. But it clearly is not. It arises in all modern discussions of revolutionary change in art and politics, and has a long prehistory. How does a new religion begin, and how is *any* innovative historical action possible?

I give only a summary answer for the present. We Anglo-Saxons have tended to make too sharp a distinction between words and deeds. An utterance *is* an action, and all action is in any case interwoven with utterances. We change reality by redescribing it. How? – Because description always involves metaphors and evaluations. When we redescribe reality we change the metaphors under which it is viewed, and therefore we change the relative values of things. This revaluation then influences the way we act. Consider for example the way in which prejudice against minorities is maintained by the currency of derogatory terms. Changing language, we change attitudes and eventually conduct. Thus Gandhi redescribed the untouchables as the children of God. It is because religious and ethical innovation and action involve the minting of new metaphors that they are so close to art.

To innovate in ethics I must change the way I value something, which means that I must change the metaphor under which I see it, which in turn means (since all words are tied to feelings) a change at a deep level in the way I feel about it. For example, society has trained us to react with intense feelings of fear, abhorrence and disgust towards the unfortunates who are at the bottom of all the social value-scales. How is it possible for a Gandhi or a Jesus to break with our normal socially-inculcated feelings?

If we were immortal souls it would be difficult to see how this question could be answered. From Plato's time onwards it has been hard to imagine how a soul that is strongly centred, a simple, immortal substance, can change. It is much easier to see how a de-centred, composite, loosely-structured and organic self may be able to change and grow. Insofar as there are in me diverse elements, often somewhat at odds with each other, I find a fair amount of internal friction and sparking going on within myself. I am internally pluralistic. This gives me a chance of shaking myself up and coming down in a slightly different shape, a chance of coming to see things differently and changing my valuations, a chance of having some new ideas. I am a compromise-formation and the terms of the compromise can be altered.

Thus if Christianity is a transgressive and creative faith which seeks to save the lowly by changing the way they are valued, it must repudiate the doctrine that we are immortal souls. 'Immortal souls' always believe in fixed, not variable, evaluative standards and always want to punish sinners, not to save them. Immortal souls are interested only in maintaining their own purity and integrity inviolate. They have nothing to gain by creative action and everything to lose by transgression. So they are of no interest to us here.

6

REMAKING CHRISTIAN ACTION

(a) Redemption and Revaluation

Ideas of sin, sacrifice and atonement are most at home and most readily intelligible in a tribal setting, where they run something like this: I cannot live except in and in dependence upon society, so it is vitally important that I respect the set of basic rules that generate the social structure and define the tribe's distinctive identity. It is not surprising that God, or the spirits, should guard these rules with such vigilance. If I break one, I threaten society's well-being and lose the favour at once of God and of the community. In this context, then, a sin was first and foremost an offence against the God who guards the sacred rules that define society's integrity and identity. A sin was only secondarily and in a rather minor way an offence against a fellow human being. The main need was to repair the damage done to society, to propitiate God and to bring about one's own restoration to favour. For so vital a purpose a standard ritual must obviously be available. It was sacrifice.

In pre-Enlightenment Christianity something of these archaic ideas survives, but in a form strangely privatized and spiritualized. It is almost as if I-before-God am a one-man tribe. I have been made by God for God, as his opposite number and his finite counterpart. I am like his child or his wife, but caught in an overwhelmingly unequal relationship with him. He is immeasurably, infinitely more holy, powerful and self-possessed than I am. He makes all the rules that govern our relationship, and before him I am always inevitably in the wrong. In fact I am continually up to the eyebrows in sins I have already committed and am surely going to commit. But totally inadequate though I am and ridiculously unequal though our relationship is, he wants me. He has through Christ and the sacraments made abundantly available to me the means of Grace. My life becomes a long struggle for self-purification. I confess my sins several times a day. I continually purge myself of past sins and seek to reduce to the minimum the rate at which I am committing new ones. My penitance grows deeper and deeper. I pray that I may die in a state of Grace. God is so demanding. I find it a puzzle that he loves me so much, when I fall from his favour so easily. My relationship with him seems to be a queer mixture of absolute security and utter insecurity. Sometimes it drives me crazy.

Today the ancient notion of sin has altogether vanished. There aren't in quite the old way any sacrosanct and pre-established rules. Instead all rules are now simply human conventions. They depend for their effectiveness upon our sociability and upon the largely unconscious consent whereby we maintain them in the daily business of life. But they betray their merely human origin by the way they change. For example, in cases such as market prices, the meanings of words, knowledge-systems and morality, change is the resultant of a very large number of small transactions. The overall consensus or climate of opinion slowly shifts. In other cases – the civil law, religion and institutional forms generally – there is some recognized machinery for changing the rules. Either way, we moderns have such a strong historical sense that we cannot help but notice that it is we ourselves who ultimately control the rules. The rules are inside history just as we are, and we change everything that is inside history. What is more, history has no outside.

It is therefore the sense of history, more than anything else, which demolishes the old theological realism and the old conception of sin as the violation of a sacred prohibition. Accordingly I do not portray Christian ethics as a struggle for freedom from sin. Rather the task is to conquer nihilism, that is, to overcome the fear that because the extra-historical absolutes are now gone, life is meaningless or worthless. The task of Christian ethics today is to overcome the crisis caused by the death of God. Christianity has to be recalled to solve the problems left by its own demise. Ethically, we must do a lot more than merely show that although the world now cannot be fully redeemed, the amount of evil around in it can still be gradually reduced. That English gradualist programme of working negatively by evil-reduction is as unsatisfactory as its Christian predecessor, getting holier by sin-reduction. No, we need to do a lot better than that: we need a programme for actively injecting meaning into life and for revaluing and upgrading people and things that have become depreciated. We have to redeem our life from absurdity by creating value, by making good, by doing the work of God.

We have been suggesting that this task is in the first place linguistic. Many people resist this assertion. They quote Marx: 'The philosophers have only interpreted the world in various ways; the point is to change it.' They quote the saying, 'Actions speak louder than words' – perhaps overlooking the phrase, 'Actions *speak*'. But actions certainly do speak, and all of human behaviour is expressive and symbolic. Not only is every utterance also an action, every action is also an utterance. People are giving off messages all the time willy-nilly.

To avoid ambiguity it might be best to use the terms 'sign' and 'communication' in connection with the view that sees the whole of our social life as a matter of symbolic expression and exchange. Words would then be just one sort of sign, and linguistic exchange just one sort of communication among many others. The point is worth making because I want to say that not only is every verbal utterance an evaluation that pressures us a little into sharing the speaker's values, but also the same is true of every sign and every communication quite generally.

Quite minimally, even if I say to you only, '$3 + 2 = 5$', I am already asking you for just a little bit of agreement and approval. Just by appearing before you, I am in some degree seeking your support and endorsement. My clothes, body-posture, facial expression and so on will tell you a good deal more about the ticket I am running on and help you to decide how you feel about me, for or against. We are always *for or against*: because every word has some evaluative flavour and every sentence uttered is an evaluation, every message that passes either brings people a little closer together or slightly polarizes them. Because, most of the time, we all want very much to feel alike, we so phrase what we say as to maximize our chance of winning consent, and in our responses to others go as far as we can in trying always to give our consent. The mechanisms involved can be seen at work in political utterances. They are the rhetorical devices used by politicians to build up and maintain an evaluative consensus among a large group of people, and they are just hyped-up versions of techniques that all of us use every day.

Notoriously, a certain amount of low cunning must sometimes be brought into play. At the Conservative Party Conference each year in Britain there is a law and order debate. Regularly the delegates, prosperous backbone-of-England types full of right-eousness, make it very clear that they are after blood. They demand hanging and flogging. The duty of the senior member of the Government who must reply to these excellent people in winding up the debate is to win an ovation from them without yielding to their demands. The task usually falls to the Home Secretary. He is reckoned a good Conservative Home Secretary if on this distinctly tricky occasion he can contrive to leave a warm glow in the Hall. Yes, he feels exactly as the delegates do, he applauds their courageous and outspoken indignation, like them he supports the police passionately, his Department is ever-vigilant and he will shortly be launching this and introducing that . . . but he stops short of any promise to birch muggers or castrate sex offenders. Yet he wins loud applause, because by fully acceding emotionally to the Conference he has created a mood of rapture in which it doesn't seem to matter that he has not actually undertaken to do as the floor speakers were demanding.

Such political utterance shows in close-up and concentrated form what morality is and how it works. It is an evaluative consensus, voiced in language, created and maintained in lan-guage, and highly coercive. We all very much want to belong to a group among whom there is such a consensus. We are willing to bend the valuations of others, and we are also willing to bend our own valuations, so as to achieve unanimity. Unanimity is very highly gratifying and it promises power. It creates a mood of self-righteous confidence that gives us the energy to frame and then to strive to implement a common policy for remaking the social world around us in accordance with our valuations.

Most of the sentiments voiced at a political party conference – at least among the parties of the Left and the Right – are of the reactive or 'passive' kind. They range from anxious concern to righteous anger. On the Left the tone is often shrill and paranoiac; on the Right it may be repressive and punitive. On the whole we find that shared negative or hostile feelings bind people together much more effectively than shared positive feelings. This may be compared with a principle on which the civil law works: behaviour can be effectively controlled by a system that threatens just now and again to catch and punish somebody, but it cannot be so effectively controlled by a system that works the other way round, by only now and again picking out a virtuous person for reward. The reactive forces in the personality and the negative emotions are more amenable than the active. My fear of punishment can be exploited to socialize me, and whipped-up communal hatred can be used to inspire great feats of co-operative endeavour such as the waging of a war. The negative emotions seem to be more contagious, and we are more responsive to others through them. They are also more gratifying, at least to the majority of people. Disapproval is a more powerful force than approval. Against this background we may safely predict that a moral code will constrain behaviour most efficiently if it takes the form of general negative rules and is backed by strong, highly-pleasurable communal feelings of disapproval, indignation, anger or outrage as the case may warrant.

Modern Western societies are populist and regularly swept by moral panics and waves of intense negative emotion. In such conditions morally-serious individuals seem to have three main options: you can be a politician, a Spinozist saint or a church member. Leaders such as the Conservative Home Secretary just mentioned deserve great respect for the difficult balancing act they perform. They seek to prevent society from going fascist. They surf-ride the waves of popular feeling and try to maintain control, guiding public sentiment towards support for tolerably rational and non-destructive policies. Alternatively one may follow the path of the Spinozist saint. Cultivate only the active emotions, and train yourself *not* to be amenable to the influence of others. Pursue love, sanity, joy, freedom – and, be ready to put up with solitude.[1]

Notice in these two cases that morality is often paradoxical. The politician is at a higher moral level than the rabble, as is shown by his willingness to save them from themselves by using duplicitous language to manipulate them. The Spinozist saint shows that in modern society you must train yourself in egoism if you are ever to be able to exhibit the purest of all the active emotions, fearless, hatefree, non-judgmental and selfless love. Only an egoist has a chance of learning selflessness nowadays.

However, these paths are for the few. For most of us the best option is likely to be membership of a sub-group, a moral community dedicated to the pursuit of the virtues. Such a community not only offers an alternative and a shelter in a world dominated by the negative or reactive emotions, but also, by being a community, has some collective strength of its own as an outward-looking and productive moral force in the world. Furthermore it actively generates new forms of life and new values, so that it is by no means a rest-home.

How far the churches are able to be such communities for their members may be questioned. The problem is that hitherto Christianity has so often been a religion of death and of the negative or reactive emotions. Inheriting from Plato a dualism which located all value in the inert ideal world above and little or none in the sensuous life-world below, and from (at least some readings of) the Bible a dualism that ascribed all value to the holy God above and none to the sinful human being below, Christianity could hardly be anything else but a religion of death. The human being and the life-world were without intrinsic value. To find value one had to reject life. The ethical was opposed to life and the ideal was opposed to the actual. All goodness came from above only.

Worse: the analogy of a political party (not to mention our own experience of small-town life) has suggested that morality is a group power device. By learning to disapprove in chorus people are bonded together, at the price of downgrading and devaluing large segments of the world. Unfortunately the churches have in the past exploited this technique in the most thoroughgoing manner imaginable. People have been encouraged to disesteem the senses, the emotions, the body, this life and the world in its entirety, so that they should look only to God and to the heavenly world above (whence the church had got its authority). Classical Christianity until the eighteenth century was steeped in world-pessimism. The world was in decay and hastening to its end. Long after the supernaturalist metaphysics and religion had declined the world-pessimism lingered, creating the moods so familiar from the mid-nineteenth century onwards: chronic mild mel-

ancholia, nostalgia, disenchantment, value-deprivation, anxiety
about transience, vertigo at the thought of death. Almost every
reflective Victorian suffered in some degree from these symp-
toms, and most seem to have sought refuge from them in
overwork. Even today we are still rather like tired old roués who
need to be artificially retrained by Masters and Johnson techniques so that we can begin to enjoy normality again. The long
religious devalorization of life has deadened our senses. We have
to re-educate ourselves. We have to allow life to return and
recover its own proper value. Instead of hating life and projecting
value out into an imaginary other world above, we have to
redescribe the world in such a way as to relocate value within our
life. Christ promised this: he promised to unify divine and
human, the two worlds, spirit and flesh. But the idea was never
carried through. Paradise was not regained. Church and State
alike found the dualistic cosmology far too useful as a tool of
power for them to be willing to dispense with it. Their authority
came from above, where all value was. You depended upon them
and you had no independent value-strength to give you any
leverage against them. They were thus *very* secure. And under
that system Christ himself ended up exemplifying rather than
overcoming metaphysical dualism. The two natures might be
conjoined in him but they were not confused, and Christianity
remained an uncompleted project, a religion of redemption that
succeeded only too well in condemning the world but could not
quite get round to saving it. So there *was* no redemption, and
there will not be until Christianity returns fully to this world and
revalues life – by redescribing it.

(b) The Will to Live

Every form of the ancient attempt to enhance the authority of the
ethical by pretending that it is timeless, and grounding it
somewhere beyond the changes and chances of our historical life,
is now at an end. It does no good to locate the ethical in a
noumenal world of moral essences, nor in self-evident and
timeless principles of reason, nor in some supra-historical
standard conception of what human nature or human happiness
or human relations or the course and shape of a human life ought
to be. All these things – reason, moral objects, human nature and

so on – are constructed within history and are subject to historical change. Our whole life is historical and it has no outside. There isn't anywhere outside history or outside life where the ethical might be grounded. And what is this 'grounding' supposed to be anyway? Is it not just one more instance of the extent to which we remain the prisoners of mythical and illusory ways of thinking that seek to explain the obscure by the more obscure?

Now if we give up the old mythical habit of trying to explain things by projecting their origin back into a timeless intelligible world outside the life-world, we also give up the old supernaturalism of reason. It used to be thought that we were rational because we had a rational bit in us which belonged to the intelligible world and was destined to return to it. Meanwhile it must not allow itself to be dragged down into the mire. Reason must hold aloof from, and must govern, the body and the passions. On the old split model of a human being, *being moral* consisted in acting out in your life a certain metaphysics of the world above and the world below, reason and the passions, soul and body. You were moral if in your conduct you enacted culture's victory over nature. Against this background our rationality was seen as being supernatural. It was metaphysically disjoined from, it was opposed to, and it strictly ruled the body and the passions. A human being was like a man on horseback, and our higher nature must control our lower nature as the rider controls his mount. So there developed an ascetical ethic of self-discipline, in which the senses and the passions were suspect as likely sources of temptation.

Since Schopenhauer and Darwin all this has been changing fast. Reason, morality and so forth have obviously evolved from 'below'. Hence a fully immanent account of them has got to be given. Our rationality consists in a certain culturally-produced ordering of the body-forces and the passions, and our morality is elaborated out of our continual sensuous evaluation of life and striving for life. Thus Christian ethics will not now begin with moral principles that have supposedly come down to us from above. It will begin where any ethic must begin, with the will-to-live and with the micro-evaluations associated with particular words, experiences and flickers of the body-forces. Ethics has got to be integral, biology-based and put together from below.

As a result our attitude to the senses and the passions undergoes reversal. Under the old world view the best sort of person was the one who by holding his passions firmly in check was able to be strong and unchanging. The male sex provided many a noble example of this rule. By contrast, if your senses were acute and your emotions quickly aroused, then you were changeable – and *therefore* a frail, weak, unstable creature, and probably female. But nowadays the biological revolution has inverted these old ideas. Everything that was traditionally associated with women – nature, a concern for appearances, sharp senses, responsive feelings, love of society and skill in managing personal relations – is now coming to be seen not as a source of moral weakness but as a source of moral strength. The very thing that made woman inferior during the platonic era, her characteristic orientation towards an ethic of life and feeling, now gives her the advantage. The last man in the world whom one would expect to be willing to concede the point himself readily admits it, for Kingsley Amis has declared in a poem that 'Women are nicer than us'.

All this, I believe, helps to explain why in the modern period the health and strength of the will to live and our appetite for life has for the first time become a matter of serious ethical concern. It was not an issue in the past, partly because until the early nineteenth century people felt able to assume that the will to live was more-or-less constant, so that there was no serious worry that it might fail, and partly because the biological will to live was in any case not thought to be important to ethics, politics and religion. Only in the modern period, the period when the State has been developing what Foucault has called its 'bio-power', the period of the great proliferation of discourses about sexuality, the period of biological naturalism and new, biology-based psychologies; only in this modern period when we have begun to think of the will to live as the conative drive that powers every aspect of our lives – has it become a serious worry to us.[2]

In antiquity mere biological life as such was not a topic of ethical or political thought. Ethics and politics started with the question, 'What is it to live *well*?' That is, they were concerned only with the adverb, the extra and peculiarly-human qualification of life. Life simply as such was not an issue, and was taken for granted. No doubt one can find many examples in ancient and

European literature of world-weariness and low spirits. Obvious examples from various cultures include the Egyptian dialogue between a would-be suicide and his *ka*, written after the fall of the Old Kingdom; the late Mesopotamian *Dialogue of Pessimism* between a master and a slave; *Ecclesiastes*; the *Greek Anthology*, and the *accidie* of the monks. Suicidal pessimism is not new and world-weariness is not new. Furthermore, idioms still in use remind us that prescientific medicine recognized that our 'spirits' might be high or low, fluctuating for reasons beyond our control. Yet I do not think that any of this bears upon my point about the very special importance of life and the will-to-live in the modern period.

For, in the first place, the modern state has certainly recognized that importance. Its sudden interest in population figures is reflected in the very etymology of the late seventeenth-century word 'statistics'. The state becomes interested in counting the population, in registering births, marriages and deaths, and in calculating fertility and mortality rates. The state increasingly assumes responsibility for the population's health and education, becomes concerned about unemployment, and through legislation extends its control over marriage and family life. The chief business of the state is now the management of the economy, and many typically modern idioms in daily use show how strongly biological is the way we now see human social existence: making a living, standard of living, that's life, way of life, lifestyle. So much is this the case that since Darwin read Malthus modern biology has become permeated with metaphors drawn from the human economy. We are so biological that we can now teach animals and plants a thing or two about life.

Secondly, since Schopenhauer first put the will-to-live at the centre of the personality, the so-called higher capacities of human beings – capacities for reasoning, religion, art, morality and so on – have come to be seen as transforms of the will-to-live and as powered by it. But it was Schopenhauer who also introduced in his philosophy the sinister and disturbing idea that the will-to-live might somehow be turned back upon itself and so destroy itself. It might become self-poisoned. It was Schopenhauer who put on the agenda the whole issue of optimism versus pessimism, world-and-life affirmation or denial, as contrasting outlooks. And it thus became possible to imagine that biology itself might fail us. I believe this was new. Right up to Malthus, who was only a generation younger than Schopenhauer, the life-energy was assumed to be constant. Times might be hard and religion in decline. You might be in mortal sin and despair. You might be tired of life – but life *itself* did not tire. It returned unvaryingly each springtime. As a Newtonian who believed in the conservation of force, Malthus assumed that whatever our ups and downs at the moral and social level, life itself, the sub-rational drive to live and to pass on life, remained constant. But Schopenhauer introduced a doubt, for if he was right the will to live could sicken and fail. It gradually became commonplace to speak of entire cultures as growing old and dying, and of tribes as becoming extinct through mysteriously declining morale and consequent loss of fertility.

Culture's response to the new anxiety about life is a more recent phenomenon than the state's development of bio-power, and has so far not been much investigated. But the fact is that in modern societies a prodigious amount of cultural effort goes into making us all feel fit, sexy, cheerful and generally full of life – and this is very new. Only in the present century has the general preoccupation with youth, sport, holidays, health and entertainment become really obsessive. To see in the media images merely capitalism manipulating us to buy and sell goods is to miss the interesting question of why it is just these images and not others that are used. After all, the products might have been endorsed by saints, but they are not. They are endorsed by rather anonymous and quite staggeringly wholesome, young, attractive, germfree, confident and untroubled characters, whose job is to link the product with the personal state we most desire, *perfect freedom from life-anxiety*. Notice too in this connection the shift away from the absurd old supernaturalist horror films towards the new bio-horror of John Cronenberg and others. The fact is that people now worry about their relation to life much as they used to worry about their relation to God. Life is the new immanent god. We surround ourselves with images of it, and we affirm and protect it in the hope that it will not fail or forsake us.

There is, however, something rather mythical about this preoccupation and its attendant anxiety. For 'life' is not, like electricity in relation to the pictures on the screen, an occult form of energy that powers all the world of signs. Life is not an immanent enabling Spirit which, as we fear, may turn against us. Life, the will to live and the affirmation of life are all constructed as everything else is constructed, *within* the world of signs. *We* made our view of 'life' and we ought not to fall back into 'theological' ways of speaking about it. When we worry about the health and strength of the life-impulse within ourselves, we should not set about fussing over it and anxiously placating it as if it were a heathen god. As we have indicated, a modern and incarnational Christian ethics will be an ethics of life affirmation; but we will not on that account seek to exploit the life-anxiety of our contemporaries, as the church has so often done with other forms of anxiety in the past. There are already quite enough people making themselves rich by exploiting the latest life-anxiety fads, and we need not add to their number. Instead we can and should recognize what is obviously the case, that today's life-anxieties have an historical explanation: they are the legacy of yesterday's puritanism, yesterday's suspicion and disparagement of large areas of our bodily and emotional life, yesterday's guilt, censoriousness and religious anxieties. We have surely not escaped from all these things in one form merely in order to re-embrace them in another? The whole point of a modern Christian ethic is that it challenges us to banish those spooks forever.

Let us then banish the spooks. The old 'theological' ways of thinking produced and perpetuated pagan anxiety by suggesting that our world is perhaps not ours at all. It may somehow *really* be quite different from our descriptions of it, for there could be out there a counter-valuation of things potent enough to overthrow our own valuations of them. The aim of such traditionally 'theological' thought, with its realism, its occultism and its reiterated appeals to ignorance and to mystery was to undermine human confidence and to make us afraid of our own shadows – so that we should become good power-fodder. But we cannot meaningfully claim that in addition to the way we construct the world in our ordinary everyday language there is some extra and different account out there of the way the world *really* is. There is no valuation of things except our own valuation. Things are worth just what we find them to be worth or make them worth to us, and there is no sense in the suggestion that there could be some rival valuation of things that might subvert our own valuation of them.

I am not saying we are right, only that there is no meaning in
the suggestion that we could be Wrong. There is no great Error,
because there is no Great Truth. Our construction and valuation
of the world just is what it is. It has been slowly evolved by us and
it sustains our common life, but there isn't anything Extra out
there in relation to which it may be as a whole and in some grand
metaphysical sense True or False. In the old realistic ways of
religious thinking there were two distinct and equally dreadful
fantasies at work. The first was the ghost-story fantasy. This
suspects that there is an objective nature of things out there
independent of us, such that it just might (*Oh horror!*) stir into
life, prove to have a mind of its own, rise up against us and utterly
confound our ordinary human confidence that things are what
they seem and our valuations stick. The ghost-stories of
M. R. James well illustrate this type of 'theological' thinking. The
aim is to show the ordinary rational human being that there are
more things in Heaven and earth than are dreamt of in his
philosophy. The method is to use hints, suggestion and deceit to
conjure up a nightmare powerful enough to frighten him out of
his wits and overthrow his normal vision of the world. That
supposedly proves that there could be some powerful spirit-being
with a rival vision of the world and rival valuations. His former
human confidence is exposed as having been sinful presumption.
Chastened, knowing he needs protection, he is now easy meat.
New ghost story, vindictive and terroristic, was but old sermon
writ large.

The second fantasy (although perhaps it is only another version
of the first) was the idea that there could be another language,
used by another being elsewhere, in which is embedded a
different and more authoritative description of our own world
and a different valuation of it. The strange thing is that though we
are talking of another being, another language and a different
description, it is yet somehow known that the description is of the
same world as our world, and that this alien description-and-
evaluation in another language is somehow able to penetrate our
language sufficiently deeply to overthrow our own description-
and-evaluation and confound us utterly.

This fantasy, when thus laboriously spelled out, seems weird in
the extreme. Yet it is no more than is presupposed by the classical
distinction between appearance and reality in metaphysics, and

between God and man in religion. Against it, Christian humanism says that things are exactly as they seem and nothing is hidden, because any supposition to the contrary is meaningless. There is no sense in the fear that the description-and-evaluation of the world built into our ordinary everyday language could be radically Wrong, with a capital W. It makes no more sense to suppose that we could be shown to be basically wrong in our description-and-evaluation of our world than it does to suppose that we could somehow show wasps that their view of their world is basically wrong for them. Our language is our language, our world is our world and our evaluations are our evaluations. We may come to modify our own assessments, but there is no way in which someone who is not one of us could show us to be basically wrong. There is no independent standard against which the supposed wrongness could show up.

From this it follows that we have no reason to go back to old nightmares and to start supposing that life, the life-impulse in us, might suddenly confound us or fail us or may prove to have a mind of its own and turn nasty. What life is, is coded in our language, and life has the value that we give it. Since the world is in language and our language is just human, our world really is ours in a way that − if we understand it − should finally deliver us from superstitious terrors and from metaphysical horrors. And as I have been trying to suggest in this book, the task of a truly modern and liberated Christian ethics is not to show people what they must fear and what they therefore have got to do. It is to liberate people from fear and to show them what they *can* do. I am therefore not giving you terrors, rules, casuistry and permissions. I am saying, you can in principle make life and the world as precious as you desire. There aren't any strictly impassable limits or invincible foes. As St Paul says, 'All things are yours'. Since Christ, the world is just human.

To make clearer what this does and does not mean, take the case of the current AIDS epidemic, which in some quarters has been seized upon gratefully as a pretext for reviving terroristic and anti-human ways of thinking. The epidemic is of course utterly tragic and horrible for the very large numbers of people who are falling victim to it. But the fearsome human tragedy does not affect our well-founded assumption that because our world is

ours and our science is ours, the epidemic has humanly ascertain-
able causes. We are confident that the disorder has a determinable
aetiology and works in some regular way. In principle then,
AIDS is surely controllable, and we will in five or ten or twenty
years control it. It is certainly *not* a terrifying unmanageable
supernatural plague.

The reason for this confidence is not of course that science is a
way to old-style objective or absolute knowledge. In the Middle
Ages the cosmos was not human; it was controlled by various
spirits and ultimately by God. *Vis-à-vis* us, it was objective and
there certainly was someone who had absolute knowledge of
it, namely God. So long as theological realism presisted you
could indeed make a contrast between our merely human and
relative beliefs, valuations and proposals and God's absolute
knowledge, judgment and disposals. But in the modern situation
that contrast has vanished. Language has become merely
human, and the world embedded in it is therefore merely
human. Instead of the old grand absolute and intuitive metaphysical knowledge of *the* world, there is now only something very
much more modest and domestic, namely *our* evolving scientific
knowledge of *our* world.

It is curiously difficult to place modern reality accurately in
relation to medieval. It is smaller in some ways and bigger in
others. Smaller, because it is just a world of human signs. Bigger,
because it is now a Christian world, that is, a world in which
human beings are at last fully emancipated from the old
appearance/Reality distinction. There is *only* appearance, things
are what *we* say they are and have just *exactly* the value we assign
to them, and no superstitious terrors can return to haunt us. We
need fear *nothing*. We are free.[3] We don't have to ask permission
nor to take precautions.

Returning to the question of the will to live, then, we have a
dual reply to those who doubt whether life is worth living, and
question whether life has any meaning. In some cases applied
science can help them. In all cases, the revaluation of life will help.
Substantial tracts of our sensibility are suffering from historical
blight. Either they never got properly developed at all, or they
became places of ill-repute, disparaged, devalued and neglected.
We will greatly enhance our enjoyment of life if we attack those
blighted areas.

(c) Making Good

We mentioned in passing that at the very beginning of Western thought the subject of physics was fairly thoroughly secularized by the presocratic philosophers. Indeed it was, but only *fairly* thoroughly, for those philosophers did keep one thumping great myth which is still with us, the myth of 'in the beginning'. They kept the equation of the quest for understanding with the quest for an origin or first principle (*arche*). The idea is that at its beginning a thing's nature is still whole, pristine and uncorrupted, and the story of how it was instituted or how it came together in the beginning will give us a clear insight into its true nature.

Science is still affected by its belief, for to this day there is a tendency for large bodies of unifying theory to be centred upon questions of origin: the origin of man, of species, of life, of the solar system, of stars and galaxies, of the universe. Curiously, these questions came to the fore around the middle of the eighteenth century in the work of figures like Kant and Buffon, at just the time when theology was turning in the same direction. A huge international effort of historical-critical research into Christian origins got under way, inspired by the hope of thereby gaining insight into the essence of Christianity. In this great quest three beliefs held by the early Greeks are still evident, seemingly as strongly-held as ever: the belief that there *are* such things as essences, the belief that an essence can be incarnated or manifested in history, and the belief that such an historical revelation of an essence is clearest at its very beginning, in the 'primitive' era.

The Western tradition's continuing interest in genetic styles of explanation is obviously connected with Western interest in hierarchies of power and legitimation, and also with philosophical theism. Everything – authority, power, value, being, order – tends to get traced up to a single transcendent Centre and Source which from the beginning makes all, knows all, rules all, and therefore is well-placed to explain all.

Lately, however, post-structuralism has severely criticized and has indeed deliberately reversed these genetic and foundationalist ways of thinking. This movement very sharply separates philosophical priority from chronological priority. Often, it says,

the best way into a subject is by a route that traditional thought
would regard as secondary, as merely supplementary and ines-
sential. Hence the celebrated proof that writing is prior to speech.
In the past, ever since Plato, the living voice of a present speaker
had been credited with a special immediacy, intelligibility and
authority. What words mean was in effect equated with what the
speaker means to mean by them. The speaker clothes his thoughts
in words, his words are animated (made alive) by his meaning or
intention, and, being present, he is in a position to make sure that
we cannot mistake him. Words voice thoughts immediately and
can be made to convey the full force of a personality. As for
writing, it was thought to be secondary, a somewhat limited and
unsatisfactory notation for recording speech and no more
essential to language than gramophone records are to music.

Derrida's proof of the priority of writing can be summed up
very simply: Although from the chronological point of view
writing may seem to be secondary and merely supplementary, it is
in fact more languagey than speech. The reason for this is that all
the common assumptions about the superiority, the immediacy
and the unmistakability of speech – the beliefs briefly summarized above – are mythical, and they conceal from us the true
character of language. But in the case of writing the speaker is
absent and perhaps even dead. Nothing is before us but printed
marks. We are much less likely when we have only a text before us
to fall into the error of supposing that meaning is a sort of active
spirit-force that lives in the words that clothe it. So we are much
less likely to commit all the fallacies, and we are much more likely
to arrive at a proper understanding of what language is, if we consistently put writing first. As for the old genetic enquiry into
origins, forget it: it can lead only to myth and confusion.

From this point the attack on genetic and foundationalist ways
of thinking radiates outwards. Post-structuralism is highly cen-
trifugal, producing its strange, disorienting intellectual effects by
everywhere putting into reverse the movement of thought typical
of figures like Husserl and Descartes. Everything that is supposed
to be clear and commendable because it is truly original, primary,
essential, selfsame and basic finds itself getting dismantled. The
whole order of things flies apart. Now difference comes before
sameness, dispersal before recollection, relations before things,
interpretation before facts, meaning before reference, super-

structure before base, culture before the self and, above all perhaps, Art before Nature. The result is a kind of objective idealism, but one which is highly decentred and antisystematic, as far beyond Hegel as Hegel is beyond Descartes.

Here as in so much of recent thought, Nature ceases to be primary and innocent. Nature is artificial, a construct, and reached only through our cultural interpretations of it. There are two main sorts of Nature. The Nature that the natural sciences are about was added on to our world in the seventeenth century as a result of the scientific revolution. Although he is only one generation before the arrival of the mechanistic view of Nature, Shakespeare still gets on perfectly well without it. The other sort of Nature has long been part of culture. It is the Nature of the state of nature, nature and Grace, and the natural man; the Nature of Rousseau, and Wordsworth, the Nature of every sort of philosophical, ethical and Romantic naturalism and back-to-nature movement. It is a literary and imaginative product, with a very strange, wayward history. It depends upon the book of Genesis and upon the impact of a cluster of Christian images and themes which represent what the paradisal world was, how we came to lose it, and what the world in consequence is now like. At the centre of all this is the haunting image of a garden-world, without evil or suffering, where the primal couple live naked, innocent and in a state of perfect righteousness and happiness.

Two Natures then, the Nature of natural science and the Nature of the imagination; both are part of our cultural history and have evolved within it. And as there is no Nature in general outside history, so there are no pre-cultural or extra-historical natures of particular things for us to appeal to. Self-consciousness, for example and in spite of Descartes, is not something original, natural and basic, outside history and indeed a presupposition of history; on the contrary, self-consciousness is demonstrably a cultural product and historically specific. That is, human subjective consciousness is formed by culture and language in different ways according to the requirements of different historical periods.

Again, some philosophies start not with the self's presence to itself, but with sense-experience. But Empiricism is wrong, because there are no original, basic and uninterpreted sense-data that are unaffected by history. Our conscious type of seeing and hearing is highly interpretative, as modern experimental psychology has demonstrated in detail. Each of our forms of perception – sight, hearing and so on – is culturally produced and historically specific. People just see differently in different periods and cultures.

The fact that our modes of sensation are not natural but culturally produced is rather encouraging. It suggests that our capacities for sensuous discrimination and enjoyment may in future be very greatly enhanced by training. Anyone who has worked with the best film cameramen, sound recordists, wine-tasters and so forth will have been struck by what can be achieved by training and practice even now.

Similarly, there are no pure and natural emotions. There are many cases in literary history of writers inventing new feelings, which may then spread like wildfire. The emotions too are historically specific. They are culturally produced and they can be trained.

In sum, the notion that we might be able to get back or down to pure, unspoiled and innocent nature is mythical. Nature is a cultural product, an interpretation; and it is particularly important that we remember this because otherwise our present programme of a fully this-wordly Christian ethic will get confused with earlier forms of ethical naturalism. When we seek to overcome the old ethical dualism of world-above and world-below, soul and body, reason and the passions, head and heart, duty and inclination, and when we seek to relocate the ethical within life, we may be thought of as being in search of an original innocent naturalness – which never existed, because nature is a cultural fiction.

There is nothing *wrong* with being a cultural fiction. We all are. But we need to recognize it, for otherwise we may fall into a bright Green nature-fundamentalism that is just as unhistorical and barmy as all other fundamentalisms. For in truly critical thinking everything is historical and everything is art. *And this is a liberating message.* Traditional thought strove to turn history into nature, to represent merely cultural productions and constraints as being immovable cosmic necessities. In this way mythical thinking worked to imprison human beings. Philosophy took over the task of being the prison warder of the human spirit with some enthusiasm, setting out to surround us with a framework of *a priori* truths, the eternal limits of the human condition. Gradually over the centuries the *a priori* changed in character. It was mythical, it was metaphysical, it was dogmatic, it was epistemological. (Yes: Kant, though semi-critical, was still a prison warder.) But we came gradually to see that the *a priori* is social and it changes historically. So, if we follow a method something like Foucault's, we shall sidestep admitting any *a priori* properly so-called, we will historicize every question so far as we can, and we will so write the history of systems of thought as to show the social *a priori* undergoing change. There are some novel histories yet to be written: how about a history of necessity, or a history of space? We've already made a beginning on histories of the self, of the body, of madness and so on. And just to read this sort of history is to feel the bars melt. New vistas of freedom open.

So a modern ethics keeps returning to the analogy of art. We cannot talk about taking morality back to Nature, or to some foundation or beginning. We are always *in mediis rebus*. We are not getting down to something basic, nor back to something pre-existent. We are just inventing. We are thinking of gradually redesigning and retraining our sensibility, our feelings, our subjective consciousness, our bodily life and our values. What we have got now is not satisfactory, so we are thinking of making something different of ourselves. That's ethics now: the redesigning of everything human because what we have inherited does not work well enough.

Since we are talking about inventing for the first time a specifically Christian selfhood (there having been so little as yet that is worth preserving) our chief interest is in the liberation of human beings. What does this mean? A human being is a metaphor-maker, a producer of symbols, an interpreter. Human beings live in language and are made of language. The fully-redeemed human life, the best life any of us could aim for, is the life that is ethically creative. That's the life that saves the world: it creates value where previously there was no value and it makes meaning by minting new metaphors. It is a life that is creative and innovative, not a subhuman life of obedience and penitence. It is a dedicated and absorbed life like the life of an artist, but its product is best described as consisting in symbolic action or communicative conduct, rather than in fashioned objects.

That is the good life, and we can invent such a life for ourselves, training ourselves to live it. We must, however, be clear that it will not be the life of an individualist; and here we need to notice a difference that the philosophy of the past twenty-five years has made to ethics. The older tradition, whether existentalist or empiricist, still owed something to protestantism and to Kant. The world was a dark place and value was posited by the heroic and free resolution of the individual legislating will. Ethical decision was by godlike decree, decision *ex nihilo*; it was foundational decision. Ancient biblical metaphors seemed still to be hovering in the background: the pilgrim came to the parting of the ways, the solitary individual wrestled with her conscience. Fine romantic images – but unfortunately you could tell that they were not very often applicable in our experience by the enthusiasm with which people fell upon, and the repetitiveness with which they discussed, a few hackneyed examples from the Second World War and from medical ethics. In real life people may very well hesitate over purely personal decisions to do with marriage and career choices and the like, but such decisions do not purport to legislate for everybody. A truly moral decision in the strong older sense was a resolution of the individual will in the face of some dilemma, which strictly implied a universal moral principle. And morality does not seem to work like that. In the to-and-fro of real life as we live it we *are* our external relations. That is, we are immersed in the back-and-forth flow of our communicative interactions with other people. These communications are all language-like, and value is carried by the signs. But the communication codes and all the signs are public entities, there already. We don't invent them on the spot, although as I have acknowledged in our use of them we are continually bending them a little. But unless they already possessed meaning and value of their own, there would not be anything *there* for us to bend.

If, then, we are our external relations, if the communication codes in which our everyday life is transacted are in their every detail public and prior to us, and if our values are all carried in the codes, then ethics is *not* just a private creation. It is first and foremost a public possession. It is given with the language and may itself be spoken of as a kind of language. It is something in which, first of all, we participate. It is our native tongue. We may be dissatisfied with it, but to voice that dissatisfaction we must still speak it. It is the very flow and movement of our life itself. Of course we may all hope to become individuals who have contributed something of our own to the common life of humanity. A new word, a new twist, a novel metaphor that creates a new valuation, the way we feel about our patch of the world and those who are close to us – and so on: some creative output is possible to each of us, and the outputs of all of us gradually change the world. But still we need to remember something that Hegel understood better than Kant, something I can perhaps put like this: in our moral action we *have* to use a language. Language is already operative as an active social force that in various ways categorizes, pressurizes and controls people, and we must use it even as we seek to modify it.[4] What we do only gets to be intelligible conduct insofar as it draws upon and expresses itself in meanings and values that are already publicly in place. My private self vanishes, it becomes unimportant when I realize that in my action I have to go out into a public language that is already laden with values and persuasions, and that was before me and will be after me. I may hope to make a personal creative contribution to it, and indeed I want to change it, but I can do so only by dying, that is, by going out into publicness so as to become available to others. The holy, the publicly accessible, the ancestors, the normative ones are those who have *gone*.

That is why followers of Christ repudiate the ideas of personal holiness and subjective immortality. We have to die to self in order to make a creative contribution to the objective common life. I can achieve objective immortality only by giving up the dream of personal, subjective immortality, and I can become holy only by giving up the illusions of egoism and passing out into the endlessness of objective life. The purpose of moral action is not to make myself into a self, but to lose myself.

(d) Boundaries

The old question of society and truth, orthodoxy and heresy, nowadays takes the form: How far are we held within an *a priori* framework which rigorously prescribes the terms in which we must live and which we can never wholly escape? Since the eighteenth century the *a priori* framework has changed somewhat in its chacacter. It is no longer a metaphysical or an epistemological framework that is seen as being absolutely immovable. Nor is it a dogmatic framework. Rather the framework is now prescribed just by society itself, especially through language. It is a social *a priori*, culture, described by the semioticians as a system of signs and by many social anthropologists as a system of boundaries.[5] (The two come to much the same thing because the boundaries are, amongst other things, boundaries between meanings.) And whether the basic elements of culture be described as signs or as boundaries, the student of culture intends nowadays to give a fully scientific account of the social *a priori*. In addition there is a growing body of historical writing which sets out to show how the social *a priori* has evolved in the past – with the clear implication that it will continue to evolve in the future. If it is a cage, it is a cage whose shape gradually alters.

So the social *a priori* can be described, and historical studies suggest that is not a true or logical *a priori*. For although there always has to be *some* structure, there evidently does not forever have to be just *this* structure. And if this is how things are, then *ex hypothesi* there are no forever-valid metaphysical proofs and no permanent structures whatsoever. The safe, minimal assumption will be that 'reality', if it is anything, is a featureless continuum. Sign-systems, or systems of boundaries and lines of definition, carve it up in different ways. Just where the lines are drawn doesn't matter. Nor, once drawn, need they be regarded as being unbudgeably fixed. But there have to be lines. No meaning, and therefore no human life, is possible except within and upon the terms of some sort of culturally-postulated order; but we cannot make a fetish of the order because it is arbitrary, variable and does in fact gradually change.

There is here (by the older standards) a curious mixture of good and bad news. The good news is that the terms of the human condition are fixed socially rather than metaphysically. They can change, so that we are a bit freer than we previously thought we were. The bad news is that the fact that the *a priori* basis of knowledge now appears to be just conventional has the effect of destroying the old metaphysical foundations of knowledge and of everything else. To those who once lived in the old order the new feels like nihilism.

And how free are we? The position appears to be that there is no wild human being. We can emerge as human only when domesticated within some cultural framework. There has to be a cage and (contingently) we are stuck with the particular one that we have got. Thus, we have no language to speak except the language that we happen to have. But this is not too bad a situation, for all that we are learning is that freedom can only be exercised relative to limits. The social *a priori* gives us a field on which to act, gives us the power to act and gives us a range of options to choose from. We can choose, within the rules. As for changing the rules, that is mainly for those rare, particularly creative individuals who are sometimes called 'the strong poets'. Certainly some people do change the rules, because historians looking back can see that it has happened. But the amount that any one individual is likely to be able to do is small. Most of us, for most of the time, must speak and act within the terms that the culture has antecedently laid down for us. And this is not too bad. Absolute freedom to make and to change the rules as we will is perhaps an unthinkable idea. Relative freedom, the freedom to choose among the range of possible forms of life that the culture offers us, is real enough.

However, there is still some disagreement about just how severe and how cramping to the human spirit this limitation is. The disagreement is at least partly political, springing from contrasting assessments of our modern consumerist democracy.

Liberal optimists claim that in the free market societies of the West a far wider range of information, of experiences and of lifestyle-options is available to people than they ever had before. So why complain? People at large were never anywhere near so free as they are now.

Pessimists, on the other hand, say that capitalism has already eaten out the heart of all traditional cultures and of all the ceremonies of exchange which once invested human relationships with meaning. Values, ethnic identities and cultural meanings have been largely dissolved, leaving us strangely homeless and anonymous. We feel as if reality has been hollowed out and has taken on the dreamlike, surreal aspect that is familiar in a good deal of modern cinema and in the fiction of writers like Pynchon, Moorcock and Ray Bradbury. Increasingly late capitalism works by controlling not just the world of production but also the world of signs. This makes it a great deal more totalitarian and deterministic than at first appears. In particular, the fabulously wide range of choices that it seems to set before us is nothing but a choice among marketed fantasies.

The liberal optimists say that 'the free world' really *is* free; we have a very wide range of genuine options. The pessimists say that we are not really free at all, because the way capitalism controls the world of signs means that nothing is now 'really' anything any more. Capitalism is abolishing what used to be called 'reality', leaving us to choose between mirages.

Now philosophers and religious people are for historical reasons inclined to take the pessimists' side in this disagreement. We do this because the philosophy and the religion of the past so often condemned the social world as a whole and told us that to be saved we needed to step out of it altogether. But the modern world does not allow us to take that route, for it says that there is no outside for us. We can be ourselves only within the social world. In our disappointment at being stuck in a bad dream from which there is no awakening, we may embrace with relief and pleasure an analysis which blames capitalism. It is doubly at fault: it is to be blamed both for the world's ills and for our loss of the old escape-route from the world.

But although we may therefore be inclined to sympathize with the pessimistic analysis, there are reasons for treating it with some caution. For one thing, if it is right how was it possible to produce it? If capitalism rules all the world of signs and we are not free, how can we even say as much? Surely our complaint refutes itself?

For another thing, it doesn't make sense to complain that 'capitalism' has eroded the foundations of traditional platonic religious metaphysics, etc. For if those foundations were really there and were *a priori* in the strong metaphysical sense as they claimed to be, then capitalism couldn't erode them; and if it *has* eroded them then they were never really there in the first place.

To put it brutally, if capitalism is really to blame then all that we can self-consistently blame it for is its having replaced an obsolete bunch of cultural fictions with a more up-to-date bunch of cultural fictions. And as for the question of whether the old lot of fictions is to be *preferred* to the new lot, such a statement of preference could only be made rationally and objectively if it could be made from the lost transcendent standpoint. So pessimism about what we have lost and been deprived of by the coming of the modern world is elegantly self-refuting. If I can rationally moan about what I have lost, then I can't in fact have lost it; so I can't rationally moan about it.

There are thus reasons for avoiding the cosy and indeed rather self-congratulatory pessimism of so many conservative and agnostic Christians. Instead we need a scrutiny of the comparative scope for free Christian action under the old order and in the new order. Since the notion of *boundaries* sounds tougher and more deterministic, we will pursue it.

In every society culture draws boundaries and lines of distinction. They structure and classify reality and they define normality.

So in *space*, frontiers, fences and walls separate the cultivated from the wild, the city from the country, the private from the public, and the sacred from the profane. Enclosed spaces are higher in religious rank, the sacred being usually fenced off. But there are also very important open spaces at the centres of cities that are specially reserved for assembly, government, justice and trade.

Time is rather similarly segmented, the various units of time linking human life with the heavens and the seasons, and alternating between sacred and profane periods. Time is unlike space in that the whole of society passes across the various time-thresholds together. Everyone passes into the holiest time at once; the transition is, so to say, quite normal. But a special feeling and small rituals may still surround the coming of a new time, as when the stroke of midnight announces the beginning of a new day, a fresh month, Easter, the New Year and so forth.

The *body* is bounded in various ways. Ritual marks life's outer boundaries of birth and death, and also the various stages within life that we pass through. It also surrounds sickness, and all passage through the surface of the body that has to do with food, sex, secretions and excretions.

The lines that divide up *society* are the most complex and important of all. In particular we should mention the lines that separate society as a whole from its various outsides, marking off human from animal, culture from nature, our people from other peoples and so on. Within society, the highest degree of symbolic elaboration surrounds the distinction between the sexes and everything that is connected with it: the kinship system, the taboo on incest, the prizing of virginity, the requirement of exogamy and the recognition of different age-sets, classes, ranks and offices.

The elaboration of the social structure proceeds in parallel with the differentiation of the objective world, the principle of parallelism here being expressed in the concept of 'totemism'. Totemism just is the ritual affinity between a segment of society and a segment of the world. And in similar ways cultural categories and classifications of every sort become established.

Having briefly indicated what boundaries are and in what sort of places they are drawn, we have next to ask how they are maintained. For lines can be crossed in various ways. Sometimes we cross them inevitably and quite non-culpably just in the course of life. Sometimes we cross them unwittingly, but if we did not *have* to cross them then our having done so may be cause for anxiety. Unwitting sins are still sins. In the third and most serious type of case an open and witting transgressor may violate a frontier. But though the degree of culpability thus varies, in general every crossing of a line is in principle slightly dangerous. Even where my offence has been minimal, society will still wish to reaffirm the line and I will still need to be purified. It is thus likely that an established ritual will be available to put things right, or at least that there will be a religious professional available whose job it is to consider the case and prescribe an appropriate ritual.

A few examples will illustrate the ways in which boundaries are policed like frontier posts, and border violations are rectified.

In *space*, ritual acts are commonly required at thresholds. Thus when I step up a grade into a space that is a bit more enclosed and holy, I am likely to be required to remove my hat and perhaps my shoes. Stepping over a line or upon a line is just a little dangerous, and stations, airports and other places that link different cosmic zones are uneasy limbos, full of little gates guarded by zealous officials.

With reference to *time*, we have already noticed that the moment of transition from one time to another – for example, the eve of one's wedding day or of All Saints' Day – is a little magical and dangerous. The beginnings and endings of special seasons and special rituals are often marked by a change of dress.

As for *society*, a quasi-ethical anxiety is aroused by anything that threatens to blur the lines defining the integrity of society and the distinctiveness of the human. Many issues in medical ethics are of this type: for example our slight repugnance at the transplanting into a human body of a pig's heart or a mechanical heart. Of the same type too is concern for the purity or maintenance intact of race, language, way of life and cultural identity. The reason why people who are emotionally and politically on the Right feel themselves to be morally superior is that they are more aware of the lines and more sensitive about threatened violations of them. The Right is that body of people who make it their business to keep society in a state of high ritual purity. Hence their basic distinction between the law-abiding and the outlaw, the good, righteous people and the excluded.

With reference to the *body*, we need only briefly mention the great ritual importance of cleanliness, dress and almost everything that enters into or passes out of the body, and the intense concern in all societies over the definition and the maintenance of sexual normality.

In many of the cases we have just briefly sketched boundaries can be crossed with impunity when the correct rituals have been followed. But a wrong crossing of a boundary creates pollution or uncleanness. Hence the very large vocabulary of transgression, violation, erring, straying, overstepping the mark, defilement, profanation and so on. To put things right some sort of sacrifice will be needed.

The whole system of boundaries is both necessary and very oppressive. Most societies permit some kind of licensed transgression as a safety valve, innocuous because as it operates it indirectly confirms the very system from which it provides a momentary relief. In our own culture the examples that come to mind are an oddly-assorted group. There is *seasonal* licence on Midsummer Night, and a reversal on Christmas Day, when the officers in the army wait on the men. There is licence under a special *anomalous object*, mistletoe. There are a few *licensed transgressors*, such as comedians, fools, madmen and Shakespeare's intersexual or androgynous figures. In the *theatre* there is the sexual confusion of the principal boy and the dame in pantomime. There is also the ritual humiliation of *initiates* who 'cross the line' at sea or join some all-male group.

Finally there is a different kind of transgression, of which Jesus and perhaps Luther are examples: deliberately iconoclastic transgression as a creative religious act. By what means such an act may occasionally stick, penetrate the unconscious of society and change the social order is mysterious.

Thus from the sociological viewpoint there are three main classes of moral action. There is the ordinary everyday sort of act which, being prescribed by the social order, has the effect of quietly confirming it. There is the occasional licensed transgression which more vividly reminds us of the normality from which it gives a brief and humorous moment of respite. And thirdly there is the very rare creatively sinful act through which the social world comes to be remade.

These three sorts of action are inter-related. This has of course been clearly acknowledged in France, where a good deal of recent theory, not to mention a good deal of time-honoured practice among the citizenry, reflects the dual belief that there has to be a strong centrally-promulgated system of rules and that the rules are there only to be broken.

But our present difficulty, I suggest, is that both licensed transgression and the forbidden, religiously-creative sort of transgression get their fullest moral weight as actions only when set against a background of strong communal belief in the divine authority of the whole system of boundaries that they violate. If the Law is not *really* sacred then transgression ceases to be anything remarkable. But in modern times various sorts of cultural and historical relativism and anthropocentrism have fatally undermined the whole idea of a Sacred Law. We know that we made the rules and it is surely that knowledge, rather than the easy scapegoat 'capitalism', that has robbed every sort of moral action of its former weight. Righteousness and sin have turned into mere social conformity and social non-conformity, which are very much less interesting. And that's why the whole historic subject of 'morality' had ceased to be exciting. It has been secularized. It has lost its ritual halo and is forlorn without it.

We cannot hope to rehabilitate the old sort of ethics, but our modern cultural and historical relativism has a by-product that we may be able to make something of. It has shown us that, at least in a mysterious, half-conscious and collective way, we have always made our own meanings and values, drawn all the lines and ordered our world. We were being more creative than we realized. The question is bound to arise: Can we in future learn to exercise that sort of creativity – making worlds, spirits, virtues, sins –*consciously* and in the knowledge of what we are doing?

The question hardly arises yet because, although they are now in an advanced state of decay, there are still around us the relics of various traditional religions. Even today we still after a fashion live in a world of boundaries and transgressions. There are still some worthwhile sins left to be committed. Only when all these relics are finally gone will the transition to the new order be forced.

Some are impatient to see the day. Thus Baudrillard and, to a greater extent, Deleuze and Guattari adopt a lie-back-and-enjoy-it attitude to late capitalism. They welcome its destructive power. Destroying everything else and then finally itself, it charges unstoppably towards a nihilism that will be Nietzschean, anarchic and liberating. Real enlightenment can come only when people are finally deprived of all the old unconscious collective devices by which they have hitherto bemused and enslaved themselves. So far we have stumbled, blinded and under a heavy yoke, but perhaps it will not be very long now before we stand up straight.

I cannot go so far as that. For one thing, Nietzsche, Deleuze and Baudrillard are obviously too much under the sway of Jewish-eschatological thought-patterns. For another, the same unconscious collective creativity that created the traditional cultures in the first place remains at work, quietly keeping them in repair, refurbishing them and so prolonging their life. In Christianity for example, the old platonic-metaphysical core of belief is being unobtrusively taken out and discarded, often by the very people who are most vociferous in denouncing us who draw attention to the process. They are doing it, but they don't want it to be pointed out that they are doing it. And however that may be, *what* they are doing – namely, their moonlight modernization-work – will in itself be enough to ensure that the ancient faiths do not suddenly collapse. In updated forms they'll be around for a long time yet. And thirdly, even if we all become critical thinkers, fully aware of the merely human character of the social *a priori* and fully aware that in principle it lies within our own power to redesign reality completely, that *still* won't bring in the Kingdom of God all at once. For the greater and more important part of the social *a priori* consists in language itself, and it is not possible to step out of our present language and into a new one just like that. Language can be changed only slowly. Consider for example how laborious we are finding the task of getting the sexist bias out of idiomatic English. We would like to bend the language just a little, but *quickly*; and it proves surprisingly difficult.

Even in a Kingdom-of-God world where free human creativity is maximal, where the old coercive unconscious moralities and religions are quite gone and where our shared humanity is continually projected, celebrated and transformed from glory to glory – even in such a world there would surely *still* have to be a common language, and to that extent there would still be boundaries and a constraining social *a priori*. And for that world to be a world of continuous joyous creation there would still have to be just enough frustration, conflict and stress to power the creative production of new metaphors. Life must not become too soft.

In summary, we are already learning to see both morality and religion in quite new ways. Religion can no longer be defined in terms of belief in God and the reception of unchanging supernatural truths. We can now see it as a continual human creative work. Since *the human* is not a given essence but something that we ourselves must imagine and realize, the religion of the future will be seen as a way of symbolizing the human condition and of generating and testing out new values and forms of life. Morality, correspondingly, will no longer be seen as the constraint of human behaviour by some set of invisible but objective, unchanging and very solemn guide-rails. It will be seen as our own continual creative production of new values. In the age of the Domesticated Man, now closing, religion and morality were thought to lay down the house rules of the cosmos and we had to obey them. In future we'll be accustoming ourselves to the idea that we ourselves make all the rules: religion and morality are creative activities, and we will have to assume the full responsibility for our own beliefs and values.

The process has begun. Already, in a small and not-very-clearly-admitted way we are redesigning our own religious beliefs and values. The ethical task just at the moment is to train ourselves gradually to assume the full responsibility for our own faith and morals. Apocalyptic talk is as unprofitable now as it always was in the past. It would be much better if we were to think of steadily preparing ourselves for our future religious decolonization.

(e) The Humanism of the Human World

In classical times a vivid individual self-consciousness had emerged only very recently. It is not surprising that people were much impressed by it, and not surprising either that the older tradition of European humanism was so individualistic. The concept of culture, the social *a priori*, was lacking. The individual naturally supposed that he could and he must take up his stand within his own subjectivity. He presumed that it was well within the capacity of self-consciousness to give him knowledge, control and mastery of himself. It took a very long time for philosophy to get around to the idea that consciousness is only very partial and by no means in full control of the processes whereby we build, store and retrieve our knowledge. The older tradition took the possibility of full self-mastery in both knowledge and morality pretty much for granted. For the same reason the thinker believed himself to be justified in doing what in any case he couldn't help doing, namely taking his own nature as his yardstick and assuming a certain parallelism between the self and the cosmos.

The modern 'I'-philosophies of Descartes, Locke, Kierkegaard, Husserl, the early Sartre and so many others have then a long tradition behind them. But they make more explicit the assumptions of individualistic humanism. They maintain that individual self-consciousness is primary and can in principle stand alone. Self-conscious, I can inspect my experience, organize my knowledge of the world, and reach out to other selves in order to strike with them a mutually-advantageous bargain, the social contract by which society comes into being.

Ethically, an individualistic humanism of this type can scarcely do otherwise than begin with egoism. The presumption must be that the soundest reason for doing anything is that it is to my own advantage to do it. However, I do not remain a simple egoist. I find the suffering of others painful to contemplate because it prompts the fear that I may one day find myself in the same trouble. It makes sense for me to do something to relieve their suffering, for perhaps I will need them to do the same for me. So also it makes sense for each one of us to support the great collective security system of the State and the Law.

This individualistic humanism was doubtless confirmed by the book of Genesis, with its picture of Adam as having been already a complete, perfect and rational human being while he was still solitary. In Genesis 2 Adam invents language by naming the beasts, before Eve has yet been created. This has given the authority of scripture to a whole series of beliefs about language, of which the two most important are that the basic units of language are naming-words that stand for things in the world outside language, and that a single individual just by himself might be able to invent the very first language of all. In short, there is rationality, there is thought, there is human nature complete, independent of language. Adam in Eden is just fine as he is. Indeed, he's perfect. But (wordlessly) he thinks to himself that there are so many different sorts of beast that it would be very handy to give each of them a name to make it easier to rule them and to tell them apart. 'I'll invent *language*!', says Adam to himself, which is very clever of him for it shows that he has got the concepts of language, of a word, of meaning and so on, even though language does not yet exist and there isn't even anyone else to talk to.

In principle, it seems, the individual self is such a solitary, sovereign being that it is prior to society and prior to language. So it can give them up; there can be wordless knowledge and eremitical wisdom.

Now many of the most brilliant and influential texts of Western Christianity – and in particular those of the Augustine, Luther, Pascal and Kierkegaard tradition – are markedly individualistic. If we wish to prolong the faith into the modern period, a humanistic age, it would seem reasonable (and basically loyal to the tradition) to proceed by demythologizing all the great Christian dogmas down into individual subjectivity. They thus become guiding categories of the spiritual life of the single individual. The old cosmic metaphysical framework is tacitly abandoned and everything is now made to happen inside the self.

Kierkegaard accomplished this and showed that it was possible to preserve the core of Western Christian faith and religious experience in a secular age. One might indeed complain that the Kierkegaardian individual becomes rather self-absorbed, preoccupied with the drama of his own inner life. But individualistic humanism is bound to be egoistic in religion as it is in morals, and the Western tradition had always said that your chief concern in life ought to be with saving your soul, with the inner life and with personal holiness. The very idea of a saint is highly individual-istic, for it implies the claim that a person can stand right outside society.

I confess that for years I followed the Kierkegaardian path and was a Western religious individualist. Now, however, I have belatedly seen the error of my ways. For individualism rests upon the erroneous idea that the self, consciousness and thought are somehow logically independent of and prior to language and society – which is obviously wrong. So when the old mythical beliefs about language and society came to seem absurd a new type of humanism began to emerge, an objective and social humanism which we may call the humanism of the human world. Hegel was the great pioneer. The world is the human world, and the human world is the world of language. Language is primary and is essentially public. Every functioning human being is such as a member of a language group. Because thinking is a silent soliloquy based on talking to oneself, it is manifestly secondary. We are first of all communicant, we are the ensemble of our relations with others, and subjectivity (so far as we have developed it) is for the sake of our social relations. It helps us to understand others and so to get on with them better. It is certainly a most remarkable development, but we should not be misled by it into forgetting that society, language and culture radically precede all individual thought and consciousness.

If we embrace the humanism of the human world we can avoid the disconcerting egoism of both the secular and the religious forms of individualism. The Christian socialist – that is, the Christian humanist of the human world – is not interested in religious experience, private prayer, personal holiness, the 'inner life' and the rest of it. That large segment of the Christian tradition which has hallowed the laborious cultivation of inner purity and holiness simply drops away. I see now that since I am merely the sum of my social relations, my life-task is not to save my soul but to lose it. I need to forget about myself and to pour out my life into the human world. And insofar as traditional ethics consisted in a lot of rules for keeping my precious self so far as possible sinless, I can forget all *that*, too. The older Christian spirituality was, frankly, somewhat unpleasant. Its legacy in modern society is our vulnerability to moral panics and to demands that the social body be purged to restore its purity.

The Christian social humanist has a different definition of sanctity. For us, a saint is not someone who has dedicated her life to making herself purer, but one who has managed to make something else better. The saint's concern has got to be shifted right outside the self. The saint is an enthusiast, a person who succeeds in making us all care more about some aspect of the world or some group of people who have hitherto been neglected or underestimated. The saint's work is to enrich some part of the world, making us feel that some topic is interesting and matters to us or that some group of people really deserve our attention. The saint creates new objects of moral concern, doing the sort of thing that Jesus did in promising the Kingdom of God to the outcast and the sinner.

The saint creates value. In a nihilistic time when the world is disintegrating, when everything seems hollow and when people doubt whether life is worth living, the task of Christian ethics is just to save the world by making things valuable and so creating more moral employment. It does this not by the dreary apparatus of commandments and casuistry, but simply by presenting us with its dual image of Christ crucified and exalted, worthless and glorious. Christ works as a symbol of the possibility of promoting something from a state of utter loss, defeat and bankruptcy to a state of glorious perfection. When we encounter someone whom the world regards as trash, we so-to-say lay Christ's image over that one, so that Christ imaginatively catalyses a change in the way we value that person. That is his redemptive work.

The contrast between Christ's two states at the opposite ends of the value-scales was perhaps better understood in early Christianity than it is now. The earthly Jesus was thought of as having been a very small, frail and ugly man.[6] Crucified, he's just another victimized Jew, and there have been plenty of those. He dies defeated, defiled and despicable. But in his state of exaltation he is as physically beautiful and shining as Apollo; and difficult though it might be to recognize the fact at first glance, these two contrasting figures are manifestations of just one and the same person. That which was despicable can become glorious. The values of things are not locked and unchangeable. A change in me can bring about an astounding transformation of the value to me of that which is before me.

The human world is so organized that it must systematically

downgrade that which is on the wrong side of every one of the lines of distinction that it draws. Losers are thus created all over the place. The dual image of Christ, as loser and winner, bottom person and Top Person, dead and alive, unclean corpse and sacred life-giving Body, has a disturbing, anarchistic effect. It effaces the lines and revalues the devalued.

It is argued by some that despite our ideology of liberal democracy we in the modern West are much more closely surveyed, disciplined and controlled than were the people of earlier times. If that is the case, a consequence of it is likely to be a widespread value-deficiency. Too many lines, and too much policing. People are likely to become melancholic or depressed, feeling that the world lacks reality, that life is meaningless and that nothing is quite worthwhile. And if *that* is how things are then we need an art-ethic, an ethic of value-creation and a subversive, ambiguous Saviour.

7

EXPLANATIONS

(a) Theory and Justification

Philosophical puzzles ought completely to disappear, says Wittgenstein. They are generated by a misleading picture, a wrong approach or an outdated and confusing vocabulary. A change in the angle of approach and in the terms used can make them vanish.

As we've been suggesting this is particularly true in the case of ethics, which is so full of archaisms and is constantly discussed in vocabularies that promote illusions. Thus many people, perhaps most people, speak of morality in a rule-obedience language which suggests to them that just as there are rules of the club and laws of England, so also at the cosmic level our behaviour is subject to a constraining universal rule-code. We need to find out what this pre-established Right Set of Rules is, and then obey them. The difficulty is that in the cosmic case there is not the sort of agreed procedure for looking up and finding out exactly what the rules are that there is in the cases of club rules and civil laws. Something has to be invented. So we imagine that the rules are invisible guide-rails and that when we are in danger of breaking one a warning is sounded by a special alarm-system in our heads, called conscience. Or we claim that the Right Set of Rules can be found in some scriptures, or that it can be worked out *a priori* by reason. Then we run into difficulties over conscientious moral disagreement, over historical and cross-cultural moral diversity and so on. Occult entities and pseudo-problems multiply – and all these difficulties would never have arisen if we had not begun with the assumption that there must be a universal moral law at the cosmic level, analogous to the civil law, and so there must also be a reliable procedure for finding out just what it is.

Similar problems arise if we make our central ethical concept the human *telos*, the Highest Good or the goal of life. The moral touchstone then becomes: 'So act as to achieve the *telos*. The best course is the one that leads straightest and most surely to your salvation.' But every teleological ethic of this kind generates the mythical notion that my *telos* is a nebulous entity hovering in front of me that I am chasing. When I set out for London, London is indeed out there waiting for me to enter it; but when I set out to strive for sainthood or my salvation, my own perfected state is not in the same way ready and waiting for me to arrive and enter it.

For a third example consider the effects of setting up ethical questions in terms of Good and Evil, the choice, the polar opposition and the eternal conflict between them. Notoriously, Good and Evil quickly become reified and then personified. The outcome trivializes morality by reducing it, as in *genre* entertainment, to a war between the goodies and the baddies.

Yet these are the three classical approaches to the ethical. The *deontological* approach, based on the primacy of obligation, puts the idea of a system of behaviour-controlling rules first. The *teleological* approach, based on the primacy of good, puts the perfecting of the self and the attainment of the goal of life first. The *mythological* approach seeks to engage us imaginatively by drawing us into a cosmic battle between Good and Evil. In all these approaches the problem is moral realism. Each approach uses a vocabulary that conjures up illusory entities, and does so because it desperately wishes there to be a cosmic moral order and scheme of things that pressurizes us in the right direction, and that will in the end reward the goodies and destroy the baddies.

To avoid all this mythology I have proposed a simpler model. Obviously there is not any moral world-order out there, *over and above* what is carried in human practices and human language, and yet somehow *backing up* what is carried in human practices and human language. We must avoid the preposterous duplication involved in all ideas of that type. So I just contrast worthlessness and value, by way of stressing that it is all up to us, that valuation is just human and that we cannot any longer look for support to an imaginary cosmic Foundation and Duplicate of our ideas.

As I have argued in detail elsewhere and here, every sense-datum, every flicker of the life-energy, every event in us is already a micro-evaluation. And language is already everywhere steeped in evaluations. Culture as a whole is a collectively-evolved and very complex evaluation of life. Necessarily, since life *is* evaluation and nobody can live wholly without value, every culture works to assure those who live in it that life is worth living. Culture must affirm life, and to affirm life is to affirm value. The higher my vitality and joy in life, the more interesting every thing is to me, the more I care about every thing and the more moral employment I have. Culture's *job* is to make the world attractive and life interesting. Culture has got to battle against greyness, despair and infertility. But not all cultures are equally successful. Some are less cheerful and optimistic, and all cultures create losers. For culture rates some things and people very highly, but only at the price of downgrading others.

Religion is not content simply to accept culture's current gradings. It thinks the overall score is too low. So religion is a systematic attempt to save the world by marking up the worth of whole ranges of people and things that culture has marked down. So far as this can be done successfully, it will greatly enhance everybody's joy in life. It will not be only the rehabilitated losers who will gain. We all gain, because ignorance, neglect, prejudice and repression make the world greyer for everyone.

Thus we reinterpret the traditional theological contrast between Nature and Grace. 'Nature' is the accumulated cultural evaluation of life that we have received from the past and which is established in our language and practices. It is very big and powerful, and not easy to shift. It is indeed so big that it feels like fact, which is why earlier generations thought of it as Nature. It certainly deserves attention and respect, but nevertheless we insist that it is nowhere near good enough, in particular because it has created far too many victims. So 'Grace' is the Christian's constructive attempt to improve the score by loving the worthless and neglected and raising their value-gradings.

This, however, is hard, because the entire cultural system works to hold existing valuations in place. People and things that are rated low don't just happen to be down; in many or most cases they are forcibly kept down. A see-saw effect is at work. Those who are at the upper end of the see-saw are up only because those at the lower end are down. Value is comparative, and culture does not know of any other way to work except by promoting and demoting, making *this* relatively higher at the price of making *that* relatively lower. The religious dream of love without hate, brotherhood without exclusion, is incomprehensible to culture. Some cultures can become so depressed and repressive, so dominated by the reactive emotions that the resultant overall valuation of life is barely sufficient for survival, and the State may have to look for ways of increasing fertility. Even in more cheerful societies the religious attempt to raise the value of the despised may arouse scepticism and opposition. The Christian, by effacing accepted lines of distinction and discrimination and by challenging what are thought of as vital mechanisms of repression, appears to be more threatening than liberating.

However, we do not all have to be subversives, for the approach to ethics that I am describing is highly pluralistic. Life is valuation, and the ethical task is to maintain and enhance the general worthwhileness of life. The value of life is not a datum: it is precarious, and we need continually to seek ways of renewing our affirmation of it. If we completely ceased to affirm the value of life, nothingness and meaninglessness would speedily engulf us. So we must affirm life. But in this we do not start from scratch; we start with culture-so-far, the received collectively-established evaluation of life. We are, however, not satisfied with it, because none of us are what we could be and a great many people's lives are barely worth living at all. So our only general imperative is: 'Create more value!' and this can be fulfilled in a fantastic variety of ways, a variety as enormous as the range of causes, occupations, enthusiasms and hobbies to which people may devote themselves. Other moralities, based on codes or on saving your soul or whatever, are much too standardizing and restrictive. *This* morality encourages you to become absorbed in enriching and putting value into any little corner of the human world that you may choose. Just about the only restriction that we need is that the positive and productive affirmation of value shall truly come *first*. Then we may safely leave to the civil law the technical question of just how to draw the limits to moral pluralism by forbidding acts that devalue either people or certain things that are precious to people. Leaving it to the law to inhibit, so far as it is feasible and expedient to do so, the forcible devalorization of life and lives, we are left with immensely wide scope for affirmative moral action to enhance the overall value of life. And in this very wide range of options only some are in danger of being perceived by society at large as subversive. You don't *have* to be a dissident.

Value-creation can take several forms. A kind of person who has often been underrated is the dedicated enthusiast, such as the gifted teacher who had influenced your whole life by her passion for her subject. Our present approach allows us to recognize the high moral worth of such infectious enthusiasm. Similarly we should highly esteem the work of artists, writers and other creative people who redescribe the world, coining new metaphors and thereby communicating new valuations.

The other paths of value-creation are more familiar. Thus there is the dedicated loving service given by a person in one of the caring professions. Such a professional's disciplined attention to detail itself creates value, and stands in sharp contrast to our own discomfort and impatience when we are confronted by affliction that demands more of us than we are willing to give. Finally there is the most revolutionary sort of value-creation, where we deliberately superimpose the dual image of Christ-worthless-and-glorious upon some despised person with a view to transforming the prevailing low valuation of her or him.

Thus value may be created by specialist enthusiasm, by metaphorical redescription, by loving attentiveness, and by revolutionary revaluation. The fourth, and sometimes also the second, of these will be regarded as subversive insofar as it challenges traditional and protected forms of repression.

Some people object that my account of Christian ethics differs scarcely at all from secular humanism. To this it may be retorted that according to Christianity God is a secular humanist who has chosen to become human in the world. When we visit an Islamic country we soon learn what a difference it makes to have a God who is human, for the God of Islam is neither human nor any sort of humanitarian, and it shows.

Other objectors find my ethical creationism shocking. They say that my comprehensive repudiation of realism, foundationalism, sanctions and guarantees leaves morality totally arbitrary. No necessity is left: all that remains is a merely contingent moral tradition and our own equally contingent efforts to amend it. If our morality is not subject to any kind of cosmic supervision and correction, we can presumably set up any morality we like. Why may we not resolve to establish Nazi values?

This objection deserves to be answered. To begin with, outside this presently-controverted area of morality and religion there is a vast range of other human activities and branches of knowledge in respect of which nobody nowadays seems to be suggesting that extra-human supervision and correction are needed to stave off the threat of irrationalism and arbitrariness. So why should our moral standards in particular need superhuman validation, when our standards of judgment in the arts and the natural sciences apparently do not? Certainly we are all familiar with numerous historic arguments to the effect that *an external authority is needed*. This external authority, we are assured, will control questions of right and wrong, maintain social discipline and save us from arbitrariness. But such arguments invite the question *cui bono*? If we accept the argument, then we are accepting somebody's right to exercise power over us. And I am sorry to say that *every* established authority that claims a divine right to dictate to us in matters of moral judgment has a rotten record.

In any case we are by no means advocating arbitrariness, nor anything approaching it. On the contrary, we have a proof. The argument is that the breakdown of all the historic devices by which people in the past sought cosmic backing for their values has left us seemingly threatened by meaninglessness, worthlessness and nihilism. However, we continue, things are not quite as bad as at first appears. For the same considerations force us to acknowledge that our values are our own responsibility. That is how it is, and how could we ever really have thought otherwise? The will-to-live just *is* a will-to-value. Life *is* valuation. We cannot live unless we feel that life is worth living, so just *in* living we have to affirm the value of life in order to live. Now the received construction and evaluation of every detail of our life-experience is carried in and communicated by the common language. It is all open to our inspection. On the whole I find that it does give me just enough enhancement of life, enough of value-pleasure, enough that turns me on to keep my life-impulse going. For we shouldn't suppose – in the naive old English nature-and-culture manner – that libido, the life-drive, is extra-cultural and a constant. On the contrary, it is powered from within culture. Culture creates nature. So culture's got to turn me on sufficiently to keep my life-drive going. And it does; it gives me enough kicks to keep me on the move. There is an interplay between culture and desire whereby each activates the other.

However, although in most of us most of the time culture succeeds fairly well in keeping life going by keeping life worth living, it doesn't do as well as it should. Too many people are needlessly condemned to very narrow and low-value lives, or are subjected to needlessly severe coercive pressures. An example that is now familiar is the massive vocabulary of derogatory epithets that are fired at young women to make them behave in just the way that society expects of them. The pressure is damaging, and it is absurd to claim (as people do) that lifting it would produce instant anarchy. Too many aspects of our life are still – often for historical reasons – disparaged and devalued. We are dissatisfied. In fact, we are convinced that the score could be made a whole lot better than it is. So religion, along with radical politics and art, is on the protesting and revisionist wing of culture. Why *shouldn't* the religious activity of value-creation be free as art is free? And we are *not* arbitrary, because our view is a modern transform of biological naturalism. But it should not need saying that our position is not that of the old evolutionary ethics, because we reject the traditional model that superimposed culture upon nature, and that made fact primary and evaluation merely supererogatory and secondary. On the contrary, we are saying that life *is* valuation. Value comes first, for culture's valuation of life makes our biological life possible. It is rational to affirm one's own life and therefore the value of all life, and it is therefore rational to strive to create a culture in which each human being and every aspect of life is valued as highly as (all things taken together) is practically possible. Such a culture will be a Christian culture.

(b) Completeness

An ethics of life, which seeks to criticize, purify and strengthen the prevailing cultural affirmation of life, will be an ethic that aims at a certain completeness. Nothing novel about that, you may say, for after all the Hebrew Bible teaches a pretty complete ethic relative to its period, and Islam to this day claims to be a complete civilization. However, it must be said that Christianity's own aims were historically very much more limited than that, and what we are proposing amounts to a break with tradition.

It is true that early Christianity did envisage a complete new world. But this new world was supernatural. It was not described in detail, and was in any case to be created by God and not by human beings. So in practice the church did no more than provide the means whereby individuals were to be snatched from the perishing world, kept pure and undefiled, and prepared for the End. In addition there was provision for the maintenance of discipline and the church's peace and good repute, by a penitential system whose operation was at first relatively open and public but which gradually became hidden and private. *And that was about all*: canons, penance and ascetical disciplines are ancient, but 'Christian Ethics' is a modern concept. It has developed, slowly and unsatisfactorily, since the seventeenth century.[1] It presupposes all sorts of things that historic Christianity just did not believe in, such as the continuing stability of this world, the possibility of effective value-realizing human action within it, and the duty to Christianize the existing social order from top to bottom.

These are all *modern* beliefs and Conservatives still say that Christians should not hold them. According to Conservatives, Christianity is an other-worldly faith. Christian ethics is a work of purifying oneself in preparation for the next life. As such it is Conservatism's natural ally, for Conservatism feeds on fears of social pollution. Politicians encourage the public to believe that violent crime is increasing, that standards of sexual morality are in decline, that unclean aliens are flooding into the country, that young people are disorderly and uncontrolled and so forth. Assiduously fanned, these fears are easily turned into public support for increased state repression. Under the cover of this repression the ruling class quietly make themselves richer and more secure, while correspondingly making the poor poorer and more insecure. The church helps by turning people's attention away from political realities and by teaching about sin and purity. Orthodox Christianity was psychologically repressive, and sexually repressed people are very susceptible to moral panics spread by politicians of the Right. The more recent mood in the church which encourages people to become politically aware is thus regarded by Conservatives as being doubly treacherous. The church has departed from its historic faith, and it has departed from its historic political function and now bites the ruling-class hand that fed it for so long.

The Conservative indictment is correct. A glance at Troeltsch will show that early Christianity was characterized by almost unlimited individualism and otherworldliness.[2] It had no political programme and normally no interest in seeking to influence state policy. The individual was wholly absorbed in the pursuit of salvation, which was the thing that mattered most and indeed the only thing that mattered at all. If the individual found that the law or state policy directly threatened his pursuit of salvation, then of course he would courageously defy them. But by the same token, if the state were shrewd enough to remove any obvious stumbling-blocks and to come to an agreement with the church, then the church's level of political awareness was so low that she was very easily manipulated.

This situation could not change until the church began to think more highly of human life in this world. The process was slow. The turn to this life began with the late Middle Ages, but an activist Christian social ethics arrived only with the first pressure-groups during the Enlightenment. These groups were composed of Quakers and other protestants, who joined forces to campaign against particular social evils. In a word, their Christian ethics was simply issue-politics; and so it has tended to remain through the humanitarian campaigning of the nineteenth century and the human rights issues of the twentieth. Christian ethics is still strikingly incomplete. You can find a Christian ethics that purports to tell you how to be an individual Christian, there is an issue-politics Christian ethics, and there is Christianity affiliated to socialism, or to the Greens or whatever; but we still do not hear from Christians anything equalling the claim that Muslims make, to the effect that given a free hand they know just what to do to build a complete and thoroughly Islamic state.

Why not? When Christianity turns at last wholeheartedly to this world and becomes a humanistic, value-creating and life-affirming faith, it must surely aim at completeness. Furthermore, when we fully acknowledge the public and humanly-constructed character of language *and therefore of reality* it becomes clear that Christian ethics must become public and political.

To spell this point out, let us consider the contrast between two kinds of religion. At one extreme the modern Catholic Church typifies religion at its grandest and most objective-institutional. It is highly political, allying itself – in a somewhat miscellaneous way – with Christian Social Democracy in the First World, with conservative nationalism and dissent in the Second World, and with popular liberation movements in the Third World. It has diplomats and a policy. It is authoritarian in matters of faith and morals, and makes very wide-ranging claims in the public sphere. It is often very corrupt.

At the opposite extreme, consider the fully privatized, consciousness-change type of religion purveyed nowadays by free-lance gurus. It is 'a non-institutional spirituality of personal insight and experience, fed by the mystical traditions of East and West', as John Hick puts it.[3] Secular politics, economics and nationalism have taken over in the public realm and all that is left for religion to be, it seems, is a private peace-of-mind technique.

From our general philosophical position it is clear that no argument-from-essence can decide between these two types of religion. There *are* no essences. Christianity in particular has no essence. It is perfectly free to become whatever we can succeed in making it into. But from our general position it also follows that the Catholic, public kind of religion is nevertheless prior. Morally, intellectually and politically one may be utterly at odds with it, but at least it is intelligible and it matters to others, which is more than can be said for the other kind of religion.

A life-affirming faith centred on value-creating and value-realizing human activity must then be organized and active in the public realm, and will aim at completeness. There are two important qualifications.

The first is that it does not start from nothing. It is always already within some existing reality that it seeks to criticize and to amend. That existing reality, which used to be called Nature and is now recognized as being Culture, presents us with a construction-and-valuation of life already in place. Language gives us a world, a body, senses, social relations and so forth. We can set ourselves to reappraise any part of this vast totality, but there is no sense in the notion that we might abolish it all at once and make an entirely fresh beginning. A ship can be patched and modified as she sails, but she cannot be entirely rebuilt while at sea.

The second and closely related point is that moral thinking must in future be conversational and not foundational. During the early modern period, around the sixteenth and seventeenth centuries, scepticism was felt to be a serious threat. It seemed that the question 'On what grounds do you believe that?' could always be re-directed afresh against any answer given to it, so that an infinite regress opened. In order to block the regress knowledge needed to be set on dogmatically-certain foundations. These foundational propositions, on which all knowledge rested, must themselves be guaranteed either by God or by their own indubitable self-evidence to reason. They were the first principles, and some kind of casuistry determined their application to particular cases. Add to this the need to systematize moral theology so that it could be taught in seminaries, and the upshot was that the church's ethical teaching was given a tree-shape: everything derives from the trunk-principles which are God's revealed and unchangeable laws, but the outer branches may be more flexible in order to bend with the winds of changing historical circumstance.

Foundationalist thinking has a long history. Defenders of tradition in a time of change, and parties seeking agreement, will doubtless always distinguish between non-negotiable core truths and the negotiable outworks of their position. Some things are on the table, and other things could never be put on the table. Aristotle similarly distinguished between those features of a thing that it cannot give up without ceasing to be itself and those features of it that are accidental and dispensable. If we believe ourselves to have some real and lasting knowledge in a changing world, we are almost bound to find foundationalism attractive. It reassures us that at the deep-down core-truth level we are basically right and won't have to change, while allowing us to appear flexible and receptive to change around the margins.

But it is mythical. One argument only is sufficient: linguistic meanings are relative, differential and historically changing. They simply cannot be held immobile in the way that foundationalism demands. So we must give up foundationalism and instead see morality, like religion, as being an evolving language and a continuing conversation. It does not need and it cannot have either certain and immovable foundations, or invisible and extra-historical rails to direct it aright. It can grow as it will, just like a literary or an art tradition. History makes it obvious enough that in these matters there are not and there cannot be any guarantees of indefectibility and inerrancy.

In the past the church did indeed claim infallibility for her teachings, but she could only make the claim with any plausibility insofar as those teachings were grounded in an imaginary unchanging world – and were therefore of no interest to us, who must live solely in *this* world. In the present generation Christianity is at last turning decisively towards this world, and the turn cuts two ways. On the one hand my faith, for the first time ever, fully coincides with my own affirmation of my life now, and I know that I am the first Christian. But on the other hand, by the same turn my faith forfeits any claim to cosmic privilege or transcendent grounding. It loses any special authority and must make its way on its own merits, in conversation with others.

The method of Christian ethics then is informal and piece-meal. It does not indulge in utopian fantasies, but rather is continuously engaged in criticizing and seeking to reform existing reality. We no longer believe either in supernatural interventions or in the possibility of any radical break in the continuity of history.

Nevertheless it remains important to stress that we do aim at completeness. In the modern West the old attributes of the Sacred and the taboos surrounding it have been transferred to the individual self. Almost without being aware of what has happened, Chistianity has allowed itself to be transformed into the sacralizing ideology of liberal individualism. Private life, the private self and individual rights are now the Sacred which must be respected and kept inviolate. The ancient priest's short fuse, his easily-provoked jealousy for the honour of God and the holiness of his sanctuary, has been transformed into the modern religious leader's vigilance as human rights watchdog. Whenever he senses an infringement he is supposed to start barking loudly. But such an *occasional* humanitarian issue-politics is merely negative and reactive. It may make us feel good but it is no substitute for the making of constructive proposals.

Worse than that: defence-of-individual-human-rights Christianity is in danger of being just a new version of the old ethical impotence and indifference to the public realm. As in antiquity, the Christian lets the public realm go hang except when it impinges deleteriously upon the individual's private pursuit of personal blessedness. The touchstone still remains the individual. And this will not do, because the world is made and everything is decided within the public realm, of which the individual is a mere offshoot and side-effect. To make any difference Christian ethics has got to address itself to the way language in the public realm divides up the world into the loved and the hated, the preferred and the rejected, us and them, the advantaged and the disadvantaged. If it confines itself to tending and defending the casualties, Christian ethics may fail to ask the critical question: 'But does the world *have* to work in such a way that it continuously creates casualties?'

If it seeks comprehensiveness Christian ethics must ask, 'Will it ever be possible for there to be allegiance without exclusion, preference without rejection, love without hate, good without evil? Could there ever be among human beings an *us* that is not held together by hatred of *them*?'

And in view of its own record, Christianity must first put that question to itself.

(c) Sectarianism

The religious dream of a world without division or exclusion is challenged by the uncomfortable fact that those who profess themselves the most religious are the best haters. Found in every scriptural faith – but, interestingly, not in non-scriptural faiths – they are the ultras, the orthodox, the extremists, the zealots, the bigots, the diehards, the fanatics, the rigorists . . . in short, the fundamentalists. They attribute their fetishism about small points of ritual and doctrine and their relentless authoritarianism to a passionate concern for – would you believe it? – *truth*. They are a problem.

In the first place we should ask, just whom do they hate, and why? It seems that they want the world to be made of mirrors so that they will never see anything that is not exactly like themselves. Anything that is *other* is dirty, sinful and repugnant to their eyes. All difference is felt by them to be threatening, but some forms of difference are especially so. There is the difference of the heretic who is like them but not enough like them, and that of the apostate who has broken ranks and left them. There is the difference of the lax person, the one who gets away with it, whose slackness is an insult to the authority of the Law that the rigorists have imposed upon themselves. In general it seems that the ultras hate to see in others that which they have repressed in themselves, so that the violence of their hatred is directly correlated with the violence of their own repression.

The demand of the ultras for sameness, for complete unity, uniformity and unanimity, is so strong that it is a puzzle to understand why they fail. Why the Babel-problem? If the internal social pressure to conformity is so strong, why has the human race broken up into so many mutually-estranged tribes and nations? Across each fully populated and continent-sized stretch of territory – North America, South America, Africa, India, Papua/New Guinea – we find that up to a thousand distinct peoples, each with their own language and culture, are recorded. Even where they are not actively hostile they do not normally amalgamate. Various cultural devices keep them apart. People who take an evolutionary and functionalist view of culture have argued that this adaptive radiation or fanning out is advantageous. But the comparison with evolutionary theory is not very convincing. Darwin's finches fanned out and took up different ways of life so that many different species could co-exist in different ecological niches on the same territory without conflict. But different human societies do not share a common territory peaceably in that way. On the contrary, a society usually claims that the sacred ancestral bond that links it to its land is exclusive.

Others have argued, along more social-darwinian lines, that cultural adaptive radiation is advantageous to the species as a whole not because it enables different tribes to sidestep conflict, but because cultural diversification makes conflict productive. Xenophobic hostility is beneficial, for it is part of a universal struggle for existence between cultures as a result of which the strongest and best-adapted cultures will tend to survive; and this, we are to suppose, benefits the species as a whole in its struggle (against whom or what?) for survival. But it must at once be retorted that we cannot here be speaking of evolutionary theory proper but only of a very dubious metaphorical extension of it, often invoked to justify militarism. And culture is not like nature. The tiger's teeth, claws and fighting skills are relatively stable and constant characteristics, genetically encoded and transmitted. They hold sufficiently steady for selection to work productively upon them. Cultural phenomena, such as the military prowess that enables a tribe to win a particular battle, are nothing like so stable. A people like the Mongols or the Arabs may have a few generations of roaring energy, creativity and rapid expansion, which then suddenly dies down. There seems no prospect of human cultural history being brought under the same forms of mathematical description as are today available for biological evolution.

The true explanation of the Babel problem is to be found elsewhere, by reversing the assumptions that underlay the way we framed the question. We assumed that unity, stability and selfsame identity are original and normal, whereas diversification and fragmentation are regrettable secondary developments that call for explanation. This is wrong. Every language-plus-form-of-life totality is in continual change. It is in chronically *un*stable equilibrium. It *moves* all the time. The group coheres only through the continual daily intercourse of all its members one with another, through which their common stock of conventions evolves. Any relatively-isolated subgroup will quickly develop a distinct dialect and subculture. Thereafter, as in a racist society or in an archipelago, only a little regular communication will be sufficient to prevent a final breach; but conversely, if all communication ceases for perhaps fifty to seventy-five years the two cultures will diverge irrevocably. If people don't keep in regular touch they grow apart, for there is no such thing as a stable culture. Hence the argonauts who are to be found in many parts of the world, from the Arctic to the Pacific. Parties of men must undertake a ceremonious annual journey around the scattered settlements of their people, because dispersed tribes have to make a regular effort to keep in touch.

The fear that the tribe will break up, that society will disintegrate and we will lose our ethnic identity may become very strong in certain special circumstances. If the nation has only recently been formed by a confederation of tribes or city-states; if, conversely, it has just come under severe political pressure that threatens its sovereignty, its religion or its language; or if it is in diaspora – then in cases like these there may be a very fierce struggle to avoid the final dissolution of cultural identity. It is in this struggle that the fundamentalist mentality is formed, and it was the wisdom of Emile Durkheim (himself of Jewish stock) to grasp how very close a people's God is to exact coincidence with their ethnic identity. Hence the fundamentalist is always some kind of super-patriot, and the atheist is always seen as a disloyal and subversive person.

Historically most of religion and most of morality has always been tribal, and to a great extent it still is. Veneration for the gods, shrines, chiefs, flags and so forth that symbolized the group's unity, meticulous observance of the rituals of social communication and exchange within the group, and the preservation of a proper distance from all aliens were virtually the whole duty of man. There is nothing specially blameworthy about this; it is just how the world was and for the most part is. And the important corollary of all this is that from the fact that religion is a major factor in intercommunal strife all around the world it may not necessarily follow that religions as such are built to be ideologies of hatred. The French language is a major factor in communal conflict between the Flemings and the Walloons in Belgium, and between the Quebecois and other Canadians. But nobody would dream of saying that this shows that there is something morally pernicious about the French language as such. Obviously one cannot suggest that French *as such* is reactive and sectarian and functions as an ideology of hatred. By the same token, from the fact that religion is very often a factor and a pretext in communal hostilities it does not necessarily follow that religion *as such* is reactive and an ideology of hatred. For it may be that something like the principle of double effect is at work: religions, like languages, evolve primarily as media of internal social communication and it's just bad luck that the closer together they draw the insiders, the more the unfortunate outsiders feel themselves excluded. No malignant intention is at work; it is just the case that those who are not in the network do not get the messages.

Oh that it were all so innocent! Unfortunately, it is not. The truth is rather that virtually the only thinking we human beings have so far known has been tribalistic and socially-determined.

The fundamentalists or ultras are basically correct in their claims and their instincts. They are indeed the super-orthodox. They are like the rest of us, only more so. Religion in general and fundamentalism in particular exists as a kind of Royal Academy of Logic. It identifies and it guards the central, historic categories and methods of thought that constitute society, establish its standards and preserve its identity.

The ultras are people who hate and repress the other, and for them this gesture of division, subordination, exclusion and repression is *the* central cultural imperative. It is not possible to draw a comparison with the principle of double effect. The fact is that rejection and acceptance, hatred and love, exclusion and inclusion, they and we, have always been correlative and coequal in a thought-system that simply does not permit the one to exist without the other.

The reason for this lies in the way the historic Logic of Division works. The world – that is, the world of language, culture and religion, which is the primary world – is created entirely by drawing lines that carve up the continuum. Every line divides reality between two zones. The upper zone, right-handed, masculine, light, stable, rational, clean and holy, is to be preferred. It is ranked higher in value, authority and reality. It must necessarily exclude, subordinate and control the Other which is on the left hand, dark, female, unstable-chaotic-wayward and unclean.

It is not just that human thinking is always at bottom binary, but that binary division always and everywhere involves ethical-ontological ranking, and political relations of dominance and subordination. We always divide us and them, the sheep and the goats, the saved and the lost, the holy and the unclean, master and slave, parent and child and so forth. This is revealed by our everyday use of the word *discrimination*. Human thought so far simply *is* sexist, racist, etc. Hence the at-first-sight-ludicrous slogan that 'Language is fascist'. We are all natural right-wingers, as every parent must have noticed who has read aloud a great many fairy-tales and other children's books at bedtime. It is not surprising that the modern attempt to achieve a critical consciousness of the discriminatory and repressive (i.e., tribal) character of our own historic categories of thought should be so widely perceived as socially subversive. Just consider, for instance, our everyday use of the word *critical*. The negative connotation is primary; we can as safely assume that criticism will turn out hostile as we can assume that discrimination will be discrimination-against.

So far, language and religion have determined our psychology and our morality. So far, all our thinking has been of the separatist and super-ethnic type that the fundamentalist displays in its clearest form. In centuries to come people will look back at our time and see it as the period when the human race was struggling to emancipate itself from the archaic sociologically-motivated thought-categories that have dominated it hitherto. We are only just coming to see that society made us and our language for *its* sake and not for ours. The primitive era is only *just* coming to an end; human beings are only just becoming more clearly conscious. The vanguard is composed of the anti-blankists: that is, all those people who battle to undo the ancient categorial devalorization of whoever or whatever is on the wrong side of some line of division or other.

This heroic battle to upgrade the degraded, and in the process to change the way we human beings have been made to think and speak so far, is the central ethical task of the modern period. Christians can rightly claim an historical precedent for it in the Gospels – provided that they freely admit that church history since then has been something of a disaster. They must join the struggle to dismantle the old cultural machinery of exclusion, repression, subordination and degradation.

It will be a struggle to reform and to Christianize religion itself, because religion has been historically the chief nursery of the thought-patterns, and the chief supplier of the machinery of degradation, against which we now struggle. For the sake of a new kind of society that doesn't exist yet, we have to sabotage the machinery by which all societies hitherto have been held together. Those who count themselves the most orthodox are the greatest exponents of precisely the moral and social logic that we must leave behind. We cannot throw them out because that would be to adopt and use against them their own categories and methods, which we repudiate. In any case they have history, the present constitution of things and the letter of the law on their side. If we tackle them head-on, we'll lose. Nor can we realistically expect to convert them, for there are no people so resistant to conversion as those who believe themselves to be well and truly converted already. So we have a problem. The struggle threatens to be hardest within the church; but the prospective gain there is the greatest.

(d) Piecemeal and Wholesale

It was presumably the influence of Descartes that made us think that just as knowledge-as-a-whole could be doubted and so needed to be reset on new and secure foundations, so morality *as a whole* may be doubted and therefore also needs to be proved, needs to be rebuilt on immovably firm foundations.

This we deny. Descartes lived at a time when for a while people felt that metaphysics and physics had to be and were being comprehensively redeveloped; and I mean, *razed to the ground* and built anew. Rightly or wrongly, that is how it seemed. But such a situation, if it is ever really found at all, is certainly very rare. More usually the position is that in any subject large amounts of material are not at present in dispute, are not of any special theoretical interest just now and are therefore quietly taken as read. Understandably and rightly, we concentrate our attention on the areas and issues that are currently important. Our arguments about method and about which way to go and why are addressed *not* to the theoretical standing of the system as a whole, but only to the local repair and development work that we currently find we must do.

All this applies to morality. It isn't necessary and it doesn't make sense, even as a thought-experiment, to propose to set aside all our knowledge and make a wholly fresh start. It doesn't make sense even as a mere thought-experiment to suppose that we could totally forget our present language and then get together to invent an entirely fresh language from scratch. And by the same token, it doesn't make sense even as a thought-experiment to suppose that we could completely demolish all of morality, dig for it new and deeper foundations, and then rebuild it as a whole. In all three cases we have to reserve some ground for ourselves to stand on in order to be able to do the work. And I would go further: it should at once be evident that there is no *half*-language, and therefore that for the debates about and the execution of any project to reform or reinvent language a complete working language must be available and already in place. But similar considerations apply also to knowledge and morality. As there is no half-language but every language is already complete, so too there is no utterly fragmented or disconnected knowledge. However sparsely-furnished it be, we always have a complete cosmology. Even while we are debating scepticism or just going mad, we always have some minimal systematic conception of space and time, the self in the world, my body and other objects, continuity in experience and so on. Although its vocabulary may be small and it may never have been reduced to writing, still, even the most meagre language, being a *complete* language, must carry within its grammar and syntax the complete cosmology, however minimal, that we always have.

So we always have a complete language and we are always in a world, and for the same reasons much of morality and perhaps even a minimum *system* of morality is always in place and cannot be wholly thought away. We are always together, for no human being is an absolute solitary. Even the hermit once had a mother. Words always have evaluative overtones, for they just are the socially-trained expressions of socially-trained evaluative feelings. Deeply interwoven with language, morality is just like language in that it is an evolved cultural product and *everyone is already inside one*. Just as every functioning human being has got to belong to a language-group, so everyone has grown up among others and has some conception of herself as one living among others. Thus everyone is the product of and lives within a moral tradition. Our moral tradition, like our mother-tongue, is constitutive of us in such a way that we cannot think ourselves right out of it while yet imagining ourselves going on being something. Yet at the same time I am also saying that this accumulated cultural stuff about us is not of prime philosophical interest. It is just a contingent fact that we find ourselves to have inherited from the past, and to be presently operating with, all these particular cosmological, linguistic and moral conventions. They are what they are, we recognize them and we take much in them for granted. In the case of morality there is a great deal of material – roughly, what is written into law codes and into linguistic idioms, and is more or less unanimously backed by public opinion around the world – which because it is not seriously in dispute is not of very great philosophical interest.

An ancient tradition has led us to suppose that philosophy is concerned with projects of *total* justification or explanation: it seeks an ultimate beginning of all things, or an absolute justification of some activity or branch of knowledge. Philosophy on this view is supremely totalizing. It wants everything to be made secure, systematic, certain and (somehow) important.

Of classical philosophy and religious thought up to the nineteenth century one may say that it was totalizing, that it had not yet discovered the social *a priori*, and that it was a decidedly infantile quest for security. But we who have discovered the social *a priori* and who understand that we are always *in mediis rebus* know that total projects of doubt, of explanation and of justification make no sense. We have lost both the absolute doubt and insecurity in which such projects began and the absolute security in which they hoped to conclude. We are always in the midst of things. Giving up the old dogmatic and totalizing ambitions, we become more critical. That means – let us not be ashamed to admit it – that our concerns become more ephemeral. We don't take up the standpoint of eternity, we don't claim to be spectators of all time and all existence, and we don't even pretend to be able to think, to doubt, to explain and justify everything. Instead we note that, living just when and where we do, we have found that certain options, issues and problems are alive for us. Nobody should bore us by philosophizing about all those things in morality that are *not* live issues. It is enough for philosophy to live in time, at a moment of time, and to address itself to the live issues of the time. In connection with these issues, it will ask questions about archaeology, genealogy, praxis and so forth; that is, how it has come about that just these issues and not others have arisen for us, how we are to understand them and what we are going to do about them. And *then* we may perhaps find that our occasional, critical and piecemeal approach does raise a global question after all.

The historical context in which we raise our present questions about ethics is of course one whose prophets were Dostoyevsky and Nietzsche. Dostoyevsky sows the seed with the slogan, If God is dead, then everything is permitted. Nietzsche declares that God is indeed dead, that there is no moral world-order and that therefore morality must be comprehensively reinvented. We must revalue everything and we must create new values. Morality hitherto has almost always rested on false metaphors, false foundations, and has been anti-life. A new beginning must be made.

We yield to none in our admiration for these great and courageous figures, and we have borrowed a good deal of their language. But a century after them it is no longer possible to talk of reinventing morality *ex nihilo*. As became clear after both the Russian and the French revolutions, the national language, cultural tradition and institutions persist through even the most violent political upheavals and ensure a very great deal of continuity. So it is also with morality and our valuations. Great though the cultural revolution through which we are presently passing certainly is, nevertheless there is much that goes on in our family life, our institutions, our language and our small daily courtesies which continues, and which acts as a kind of ballast. All this material does much to secure the continuity of our social life and our practice, but as has been said it is contingent and customary, and we should not waste our efforts in struggling to find or construct metaphysical foundations for it. A critical moral and social philosophy is not concerned with fabricating specious justifications for what, in the last analysis, merely happens to be so. Philosophy comes in only when we start wanting to change things. Most of the time you and I are content enough to go along with that vast accumulated system of improvised, conventional valuations and practices that we call our way of life. We go along with it, it just is what it is, we like it as it is and we are not complaining about it. But start to want to *change* things – and philosophical issues raise their heads.

We took from the late-nineteenth-century pioneers the idea that the vital issues in modern ethics have to do with the worth of life. Questions about our duties and about divine commandments are not of interest now. They date from a time when there was an objective moral world-order and moral values and requirements were seen as being somehow constituents of reality. Just as the mind in knowledge conformed itself to an intelligible order out there, so the will in morality conformed itself to a moral order out there. You fitted into your niche, learned the rules and did what was demanded of you. Somehow you accepted that the whole scheme of things had a *right* to tell you what to do. The Universe was like a vast well-ordered house with roles and rules laid on for everybody. It was a servants-and-masters vision of the universe, and when it died people were at a loss. When there was nobody telling them what to do any more, people felt the world was empty and meaningless – and so our question about the worth of life came to the forefront of interest. Rather similarly, the newly-emancipated American slaves after the Civil War are said to have felt a sense of *anomie*, and for a time seemed to be worse off free than they had been when in bondage. And insofar as all this is so then even today, a century on, there is still a good deal of philosophical interest in the question of how it is that we human beings are able collectively to project value into life. How can we strengthen this capacity, how can we upgrade the value of areas of our life that have become somewhat run down, and *what in any case are the limits?*

The older Christian ethics, timorously preoccupied with purity, penances and rules, with precedents, permissions and safe limits, was absurd and is obsolete. But the newer Christian ethics is more interesting and more evangelical. It wants to preach good tidings to the poor. Its aim is to put more value into life by seeking to improve the image or raise the status of whatever is at present neglected and disparaged. This work can be seen as a linguistic task. Our words are the expression of our feelings and the vehicles of our valuations, and they are intimately bound up with our practice. The way we talk about (just for example) gypsies shows the way we feel about them and the way we will end up treating them. So if we think that the gypsies are getting a raw deal then we've got to find ways of redescribing them, getting people interested in their culture and their history, and changing the way people feel about them. And if we can bring it about that everybody likes and respects the gypsies a bit more and gives them a better deal, then the overall value of life has been slightly increased for everyone. We've done something good which needs no further justification. For us humans life *is* valuation, and our affirmative valuations are just life's own self-affirmation in us. When we say Yes to something then life says Yes to itself – provided only that our act of affirmation be spontaneous and outwardly directed. If we take an external-relations view of the self, as we do, then the purification of the inner me is not an interesting ethical goal. Instead we should see the ethical theatre as being the objective human world, the world of public meanings, values and social relations. Following Christ, my life-task is to get a bit of added value into that world. Our personal 'holiness' should be of no interest to us, but we ought to love the life-world. By the way we love the human world and prize each corner of it we make the world a bit more real for everyone, and *that* is what is needed.

We may be very pluralistic in our view of the good life. I am quite ready to congratulate you if you have devoted your entire life to the advancement of the game of croquet; but since games are only games and the real world is the human world, it is not surprising that a Christian should rank humanitarian values highest. By that I mean just that the most important of our valuations is simply our valuation of each other. But now look to your language. Look at the terms that you use with the strongest overtones of repugnance or distaste. The best Christian life is the life that is dedicated to those who are of the least account, those who are the most victimized – and your own vocabulary will give you a pretty good idea of who they are.

Thus the new Christian's piecemeal approach says that after the end of the old moral world-order the worth of life is up to us. Your life-task is to create a bit more value (which equals, a bit more reality) for us all, by inducing us all to speak a bit more kindly of something or other – preferably something human and preferably something that is having a bad time and is the victim of prejudice.

Now, however, we see that the piecemeal approach may lead us to perplexing and difficult large-scale problems. Let us return to the gypsies. People began to live the settled life at the time of the Neolithic Revolution around 12,000 years ago, and ever since there has been conflict between Cain the settled man, the agriculturist, and Abel the man of no fixed abode, the nomadic pastoralist. When a modern publican in Kent refuses to serve a gypsy, he is re-enacting a hostility of the settled man towards the nomad that goes back perhaps ten thousand years. Cain's murder of his brother Abel is the archetypal myth, suggesting why for so long the travelling tinker, the vagrant, the wayfarer, the nomad and the gypsy have been looked down upon and regarded as dirty, thieving and shiftless.

We are not here talking only about a mere non-rational emotive reflex or gut reaction, such as a phobia or an irrational dislike. In our philosophy there is no very clear line between reason and the passions *anyway*, and around the world the settled man's hostility to the nomad has percolated through morality and metaphysics until it has become very deeply inbuilt. It is now part of the structure of thought. Language has become permeated with a strong preference for whatever is stable, upright, reliable, fixed in one place, and can be counted upon to be there when you need it and to come when you call for it. At various times in our European past, indeed, Bishops were debarred from translation. They had to stay in one diocese, as monks were supposed to stay in one monastery and as couples normally remained for life in the house built for their marriage. Stability was reckoned a virtue and even a sign of blessing. Conversely, the nomadism imputed to 'the Wandering Jew' was the symbolically appropriate fate of one who was regarded as being accursed and condemned to be a fugitive like Cain (Gen. 12).

All this means that language itself is stacked against the unlucky gypsies. Any effort we make on their behalf will be countervailed by a heavy linguistic drag that all the time tells against them. For the general rule is that every people's language is saturated with evaluations that put them at the centre of their own world, that make their own way of life seem to them to be the norm, and that act to preserve their own culture's ethical-ontological rankings. We began with the gypsies only because they are a relatively unfamiliar example. Other cases have become so well-understood that we scarcely need to say that language is tilted against those whose misfortune it is to be lower-class, black, female, gay, handicapped or whatever. Until as recently as the 1960s philosophy still clung to a sharp distinction between the world of fact and the world of value. Now, it seems astonishing that so recently people could not see the obvious: language is so steeped in valuations that most of what people say, most of the time, is acting to ratify the evaluative consensus that is embodied in the social order – its institutions, its hierarchies, its power-relations. The concrete social order of a people, their everyday language and their morality are just three aspects of the same entity. It is a very large and complex entity, still not well understood. It changes indeed, but it also has powerful mechanisms of daily self-confirmation and self-defence.

As a rough guide, the greater the moral importance of the cause you take up the more active will be the resistance you encounter.

Thus in terms of our earlier examples, if you dedicate your life to the advancement of the game of croquet you may meet some passive resistance, in the sense that people will lazily go on thinking of croquet as a comically genteel game, but you will not stir up much real hatred. By contrast, if you make serious efforts to find more camping sites and school places for gypsies then you will meet fierce opposition from people determined not to have a gypsy caravan near their own home or a gypsy child in the desk next to their own child at school. The fierceness reflects the strongly negative valuation of the gypsies and their way of life that is built into our language and our ways of thinking.

Such things are not easily changed, especially in cases where people feel that values of survival are at stake. Consider the case of those gays who want homosexual practices and unions to be given the fullest parity of social endorsement. To the average heterosexual it is hard to see how this can ever be fully conceded. An ethic of life *must* favour reproduction, must prefer fertility to sterility. Society must surely tilt the balance of language and valuation towards its own survival – which means towards encouraging the sexes to like each other, encouraging heterosexual unions and the begetting and careful raising of children. The gays themselves are the products of heterosexual unions, and are themselves well aware that it is not always easy for the two sexes to get on together. The sexes need incentives, and society's bias towards heterosexual marriage is in society's interest. Yet some gay rights groups appear to be asking for more than toleration, more than respect and more than equal rights. They want equally active backing, or what I am calling full parity of social endorsement, as if society could just as well be 90% gay as 90% straight. Could it? Does not this raise the question we put earlier: *What are the limits to the extent to which everything can be affirmed?* Does it make sense to suppose that society could equally warmly recommend settled life and vagrancy, heterosexuality and homosexuality, and so on? Surely someone who is benignly and indifferently pro-everything ceases to be really pro-anything?

What happened historically, and continued to happen pretty effectively until about the time of the Industrial Revolution, was that our culture like others was dialectical. It contained opposites and made limited provision for the reversal of even its more important valuations. There was thus a safety-valve, and the themes of value-reversal and conversion were prominent in scripture, ritual and symbolism. Christ might be a king but he was also a poor man; he might be secure on his throne but, like his early Apostles and Francis, he had been an itinerant. At its best Christendom was more of a civilization than a system. Like a language, it was a symbolic resource versatile enough to be invoked in the service of an indefinitely wide range of causes and interests. It had a great deal of spiritual space and room for movement inside it. Thus although it might still be true that the evaluations dominant in the language were tilted against the gypsies, there was also plenty that you could appeal to if you wished to promote their cause. The culture was *both* tilted into a dominant shape *and* so ordered as to permit a measure of deviance.

How well arrangements of that type worked may be disputed. No doubt there was much variation. In any case, everything is now changing. *We are losing our old capacity to create and maintain a coherent order that embodies and confirms our values.* This astounding and catastrophic event was detected by Nietzsche, who ascribed it principally to the growth of critical reflection, steadily undermining the old unconscious machinery by which in the past values had been posited and maintained. Now we know how we did it, we can't do it any more. Alternatively the loss of value may be ascribed either to our modern equal-rights multiculturalism which entails relativism, or to the capitalism which weirdly takes away real values and puts in their place just – *images* of values. Whichever explanation be preferred (and probably Nietzsche's is nearest the mark) we cannot expect ever again to see values embodied in the social order and its institutions with quite the old assurance and clarity. Still less will the old reversals, licensed transgressions and the like ever to be set up again in quite the old way. A true society, in the old sense, cannot now be restored. In the long run we are going to have to create something new.

We do not care at all for the prospect. We look at the prototype planned societies of Eastern Europe and we shudder. They seem horrifically impoverished in comparison with the old order that they replaced, and of which (we flatter ourselves) something remains among us in the West. But the truth is that almost nothing is left of the West and, impoverished and unjust though they be, those planned societies of the East still represent our first, though utterly unsatisfactory, attempts to create a future.

The old pre-twentieth-century type of society was value-rich at the price of creating a lot of losers. The lines that defined the various normalities so clearly were lines that also excluded many heretical, deviant, deprived and sinful minorities. We would feel much less regret about the final disappearance of that type of society if we felt confident that we could see how to build a new sort of society which has clear values without doing so much excluding as the old one did. We would like to know if it is possible in the future to build a society more comprehensively affirmative than any that we have seen so far.

(e) Mediation

On our account, good deeds are both indefinitely diverse and minutely particular. Because we cannot live unless we feel that life is worth living, life's struggle for life takes in us human beings the form of a struggle for value. A lonely old person keeps a dog to give herself a reason for living; and let us be truthful, we are all of us like that. It need only be added that merely private cherishing is not quite enough. You must strive to put your own small corner of things on the map by raising a little the general public estimation of its value – of which a reliable index is the way it is spoken of in everyday language. The most important of our valuations is our valuation of each other, and the most striking and important act of revaluation we can accomplish is sharply to upgrade the public valuation of some group of human beings who are currently despised.

The common talk nowadays is of rights. One battles for human rights, or even for animal rights. But this talk of rights is too often mythical. It gives people the impression that a right is a queer, non-objective but empirical property that a thing just has by nature, whether it has yet been recognized or not. I want to avoid mythicizing rights in that way, so I use a more modest terminology. If I battle on behalf of some group's 'natural' moral rights, I am simply trying to get people in general to speak more highly of that group and to treat them more kindly. If I battle on behalf of their legal rights, then I am simply trying to get that improved treatment of them protected by law. Full-blown talk of rights is 'theological', and many people are still very much attached to ancient theological ways of speaking. Nevertheless there is a strong case for renouncing such theological idioms. We live in a period of very rapid change in which talk of 'natural rights' as changeless, extra-historical, objective moral properties is highly unconvincing, and moreover we live in an age when much of our life and our world is beginning to suffer headlong devalorization. People fear that life is becoming shadowy and worthless. The world is all flickering images, and there is a marked shortage of reality. In extreme cases people are becoming very depressed, or even withdrawing into a numbed schizoid condition. In this cultural context we need to remind ourselves that the remaking of value and the infusion of worth into every corner of the human world is up to us. We can do it; it is a work of the human creative imagination, an ethical work to which everyone can contribute something. The mythical talk of rights gives the impression that the worth of things is an antecedently-fixed and unchangeable quantity. That is just wrong. The worth of things waits to be assigned to them by us and can be fixed at a level of our choice. If the overall value of things has slipped, that's our fault, and we can put it up again if we try hard enough.

However, it has already become clear that my own particular ethical deed cannot stand alone. If it is to be delivered from absurdity it needs to be taken up into some larger whole. There needs to be some kind of mediation between the particular and the universal, and on various axes.

First, as I have suggested, our view of ethics is very pluralistic. Everyone needs to be an enthusiast for something or other, but the range of possible good causes is indefinitely large. Only a very few of the greatest artists can produce work of such vast imaginative scope that it celebrates and enhances life-as-a-whole. The rest of us must specialize, and to such a degree as to risk absurdity: how, we wonder, can a whole life dedicated to such-and-such possibly be a good life? To overcome this sense of absurdity the individual needs to be able to see herself as belonging to a larger community whose entire production taken together is ethically comprehensive. Her little work is saved from absurdity by being incorporated into a whole to which it contributes and from which it draws meaning.

In the last section we met a *second* way in which there may be some conflict between the particular and the universal. Christian ethics, we said, seeks to change things. It doesn't quite set out to create value *ex nihilo*, but rather is interested in revising some current valuations – the point being that in the language and in our current social order and social practices there is a very detailed evaluation of life already in place. So the Christian embarks upon the very specific task of attempting to upgrade just one thing (we instanced the status of the gypsies) – and soon learns a painful lesson. Society's current set of valuations is a loose-knit but very large and interlocking whole which is entrenched and which acts to confirm and defend itself. After banging his head against a brick wall for some time, the Christian may begin to suspect that you cannot hope permanently to change the value of anything unless you first change everything. So the second universal-particular axis is that between doing a good deed in some minute ethical particular and seeking a revolutionary change in the whole social order.

The *third* universal-particular axis is the newest and most fearsome. In the modern period we have lost the old and wonderful belief that history or the long run or the universe or something is on our side, so that when we act rightly we act in tune with the deepest nature of things. Of a good man it used to be said that he was on the side of the angels. So there *was* a right side, and good deeds were not utterly forgotten. The cosmos was thought to endorse goodness. But Jesus, dying, learned that this was not the case. He was not rescued but was left to cry, 'My God, my God, why hast thou forsaken me?', and we modern Christians who have died with him have echoed his words and have learnt that he is right. There isn't any cosmic endorsement. So there needs to be mediation between the moral strivings of the individual and their larger background – especially in an age when large-scale historical forces are at work actively destroying value much more rapidly and thoroughly than we can hope to restore it. We are fighting a losing battle *twice over*. The cosmos is not on our side, and history is not on our side. But we can side with each other.

Mediation on the *first* axis is fairly straightforward. The individual needs to belong to an ethical community, and fully to do its job of saving the narrow specialized life of the individual from absurdity, the community should be large, plural, spacious, generous and catholic. Its overall valuation of life, as expressed in its whole communicative production, must be rich and diversified. Does it need to be systematic, or even internally self-consistent enough to be in principle capable of systematization? Great art suggests not. We desire system only insofar as we wish to see some Monarch's power magnified. Life itself is unsystematic.

It would be facile to claim that the church still does provide, or even that it *can* any longer provide, the sort of larger community people need to be part of. Maybe at one time it was big enough, but Hegel's philosophy marked the arrival of an age when people would look for moral fulfilment to the State rather than the church, and nationalism was to become a stronger force than traditional religious belief. Since the beginning of the nineteenth century the church has become very narrow, and the State is turning – has often turned – into a value-destroying and monstrous machine. Just at present it seems that people identify themselves most closely with near-at-hand and small-scale neighbourhoods and institutions. Alasdair MacIntyre has argued that we need to create new local forms of community in which the moral and intellectual virtues and values can be conserved during the new Dark Age which has already begun.[4] The parallel is with the achievement of the Monastic Order between the sixth and tenth centuries, but there must be doubt about whether anything similar is feasible today.

The *second* axis ran from doing a good deed in some very particular case to seeking a revolutionary change in the entire social order. Suppose for example that I join the movement for the ordination of women and pay my subscription. Suppose indeed that I manage to do a few more things than that; still, as everybody knows, no particular act in the cause of the full equality of women can *stick* under present conditions. After a hundred years and more of struggle, of small victories and concessions, we can see that most of the battles have been won by now and most of the argument is won – and yet, from another point of view, how little has changed! And is it not a familiar puzzle in relation to almost every great ethical struggle nowadays, that you can win all the battles and then discover that you still haven't won the war? To an empiricist it must be bewildering to find that after each and every tree has been chopped down, the wood still stands. It would be enough to set us dreaming of revolution, were it not that the same disappointing paradox often arises nowadays in relation to revolutions also.

Can moral action – which, remember, means for us action to change publicly-agreed valuations – really stick and make a lasting difference, or does socio-linguistic drag always return like the tide and wash away all we have tried to do? At this point religion really does help, so much so that even those who do not practise it must call upon its language. It is a tenacious rememberer, collecting our endeavours and consolidating them into traditions which it guards and perpetuates. Still more important, religion simultaneously insists on the importance of the next step, the one-off action, *and* holds before us images of the radical transformation of the self and the world. It surrounds the moral life with a supportive symbolic and institutional context.

These considerations are taken a great deal further on the *third* axis, that which runs between our individual strivings and their blankly indifferent or actively hostile cosmic backcloth. Religion has a most mysterious power to draw moral strength from tragedy. The Jews draw strength from the contemplation of their ruined Temples, their exiles, their martyrdoms, and their long history of persecution and flight. Shia Muslims to an astonishing extent are *nourished* by the martyrdom of Ali, and Christians (especially in the present century) by Christ's self-identification with the defeated in his death.

It is strange that the centre and mainspring of religion should in these three cases be an image of the triumph of evil and the failure and defeat of the righteous. Why should faiths that are widely believed to teach optimistic monotheism actually centre around images of the straight *falsification* of realistic belief in a good and powerful Providence? Nietzsche suggests that the religious spirit is vengeful and reactive and that it continually reinforces itself by brooding over ancient grievances. This must be wrong, because the observances at the great festivals of the three faiths simply cannot be read as chiefly designed to stir up hatred. The Good Friday worship of Christians has in the past sometimes been exploited – and even worded – in the interests of antisemitism, but this was never demonstrably the real logic of the ritual at the Mass of the Presanctified. When religion commemorates a martyr – Jesus, Ali, Akiba, etc. – it lays the main emphasis upon the suffering of the victim rather than upon the identity of the persecutors. We do not leave Good Friday worship seething with anger at Roman soldiers. It seems rather that when religion makes us identify ourselves with a martyr its aim is dionysiac. We experience the worst. We are plunged into the primal terror of existence and the eclipse of consciousness by pain, evil and death, and we are thereby purged. We emerge from the ritual having undergone the worst there is, and ready now to accept from moment to moment the pure gratuitousness of life. Ready too in morality to do what needs to be done by us in a spirit of gratitude rather than complaint.

Thus religion mediates between the particular and the universal in the moral life – and can in principle continue to do so even after we have come to accept a thoroughly anthropological and symbolist interpretation of its rites and teachings.

8

POLICIES AND PERSONALITIES

We have rejected and avoided all those accounts of morality, supernatural and heteronomous, that picture the ethical as a hidden super-authoritative Demand of which we are intuitively aware. We used to think we could sense it pressing upon us, constraining us and causing us to have very bad feelings if we did not obey its dictates. That was how morality once felt; but that ethical psychology has now died on us, and we have no option but to reject as mystifying and meaningless much of the traditional vocabulary of morality. I am not interested in personal purity or in code-morality. You will not here find me deducing a set of rules for you either from the nature of practical Reason, of from human nature, or from Revelation. We do not propose to work out a tree-structure of general principles and more particular applications, of commandments and casuistry, of statute law and case-law. Nor are we here preoccupied with questions of personal sin and forgiveness. No doubt a great deal of material of that sort has come down to us from the past and has such weight that it is in effect part of us, but even so I would prefer us to think of it all as being merely contingent. It is just a fact, and no more than a fact, that our moral tradition happens to have evolved in the way it has and to have left us with the legacy it has left us with. We may sort through it and find many nuggets, but we need not mythicize it nor credit it with any more systematic coherence than in fact it has (which is not much).

But, you may object, if we are so resolutely non-directive, if we flatly refuse to provide a code or any detailed guidance, then are we not uselessly vague? No: and chiefly because modern social life is highly psychological. There is among us a spectrum of psychological types which is rather closely correlated with the political/ethical spectrum. We are so psychologically-minded that when we know what kind of person a Christian is – that is, when we have grasped how the Christian self should now be constituted, the techniques, the practices and the mode of development of selfhood, and the self's relation to life, to time, to others and to feeling – then we have all we need. The moral and social policies of such a self can be guessed with quite sufficient definiteness, in much the same way as you know soon after meeting people how they vote and which newspaper they are likely to prefer.

This important fact about modern culture explains the fascination during the past thirty years of the project of a synthesis of Marx and Freud. We feel that a detailed theoretical matching of the range of political with the range of psychological types must surely be within our reach. And this confidence is probably inherited from Christianity in general and Protestantism in particular. In effect the Protestant said: if your faith is right, then the right sort of works will flow from it without difficulty. Generalize the principle, and we can lay down the rule: from your form of selfhood your general moral outlook, values and policies can be inferred.

It now becomes a little clearer why in the present text we have linked together a certain form of ethical naturalism and a strong emphasis on moral creativity and freedom. In rejecting ethical supernaturalism we refused to regard the ethical as something autonomous, distinct from and over-against nature, and having its own structure and laws. Ethics on our account is not a separate science with a special method of its own and its own unique subject matter. And hence we reject system. To make ethics systematic you need to start with either a clear fact-value distinction (to give you the necessary autonomous ethical realm), or a rather sharp-edged picture of the perennial moral constitution of human nature, or both – and we have neither. Every autonomous discipline looks for a distinctive structured subject-matter and method of its own, so that it can keep out intellectual poachers and build itself up into a science; and we have rejected such a view of ethics. We know that the self can be constituted in many different ways and that these different constitutions of the self are different constitutions of its emotional dynamics. Each such constitution just *is* an ethic, because our emotions just *are* our evaluations. So ethics is not anything quite separate from the general field of the social and psychological sciences. Furthermore, on our account Christianity is a religion of redemption. It teaches that the prevailing valuation of life, as expressed in our present forms of selfhood, ways of speaking and social practices, is far too low, low enough even to threaten our long-term survival. We are not getting enough out of life, nor are we putting enough into it. We fall so far short of what we should be that we are in danger of nihilism: such, translated into intelligible language, is the historic Christian message. It continues by offering us a path to redemption modelled on the exaltation of the rejected and slain Jesus. The way to salvation is by actively striving to push up our values, and ennobling everything that is currently rated too low. But for this work of redemption we don't need a system. We don't want conscience, rules or guilt. We need freedom, creativity and vigorous active emotions.

Those moral theorists who seek to systematize morality are acting in effect as the agents of the morality we now have. They are trying to increase its power over us and correspondingly to reduce our scope for creativity and the exercise of our freedom. They are wrong, because the ethic we've got won't do. It is too often an ethic of death, reactive and repressive. To redeem our life we must create new values fast. That in turn means that the Christian has to be like an artist – and one simply cannot legislate *a priori* to an artist. Therefore, no system.

But we do have a Christian form of selfhood, which readily leads to a view of life and a general policy for life. Let us begin by considering our relation to marxism.

On a number of major issues we are evidently still marxists. Our philosophy of language led us away from the soul and individualistic humanism towards an external-relations view of the self and a thoroughly 'common' or social humanism. This we called a humanism of the human world, a phrase which of course was borrowed and adapted from the young Marx.[1] It is a secular humanism, because according to Christianity God has chosen to become a secular humanist – that is, a human being within the world – and what is good for him ought to be good enough for us. And because we have now committed ourselves to this world as completely as God himself has done, we also say Yes to Marx's radical historicism. Yes, the whole of our life really is lived inside history, so that the supposed sciences of the *a priori* realm such as mathematics and logic are just as much developed within history by human beings, and subject to historical change, as are the empirical sciences. And Yes, too, our moral and religious thought is also thoroughly intra-historical. We agree with the marxists in rejecting idealism and transcendence, where those terms are used in such a way as to imply a claim that there is a bit of us that is not historical and which has the capacity to grasp extra-historical truth. That idea is illusory, as becomes clear to anyone who reflects on the way thought is transacted in language.

Finally we also go along with the marxists in their very just sense of the subtle interconnection of everything human within the whole web of culture. We feel the web historically when we grasp, for example, how completely Victorian everything Victorian is, and we feel the web presently when we study the English dictionary – for the book *of* the language is the single most instructive work *in* the language.

We are so close to the marxists because theology has become so very historical a subject, and because modern culture just is a lot more marxist than it (often) cares to admit. But there are differences, too. The route by which we approached marxism (language, the external-relations view of the self, radical historicism) has also shown us that there is a great deal wrong with classical marxism. Especially all the left-over Enlightenment elements in it; for if we really do accept radical historicism and a post-structuralist understanding of language then we reject the idea of progress (because there is no extra-historical yardstick to measure it by), and therefore we reject also marxist optimism (for nothing says that things must get better, and there's no yardstick for measuring that 'better'). Therefore too we reject the marxists' Enlightenment scientism, for the endlessness and indeterminability of meaning and interpretation rule out the idea of fully objective and assured knowledge. Accepting our own thoroughgoing historicality, we also disclaim a certain residual essentialism that can be detected in Marx's notion of the human *Gattungswesen* or 'species-being'.[2] He felt he couldn't speak of human liberation or fulfilment without invoking such an idea, but insofar as it functions in his thought as a supra-historical guiding star, a yardstick and a goal, it is a bit of platonism and we must learn to do without it.

Our last disagreement with Marx is one familiar to readers of Foucault. In their discussions of power Marx and his followers have concentrated too much on its largest-scale and most centralized manifestations – the power of the state, the economic system and the dominant class. They neglected something else that matters just as much in the lives of most people, namely the 'micro-power' exercised daily in the smaller institutions. Of these the family is the most basic, and here we need to consider, for example, the power exercised by men over women and by adults over children. Marxism has been relatively weak or inconsistent in these areas. Christianity, it might be retorted, has not got any too good a record either, but because its greatest strength since the Reformation has lain in the sphere of face-to-face relationships it is well placed to get the message. As a result, American Christians today often grasp micro-power issues much better than do Russian Communists: compare for example their responses to AIDS, feminism, children's rights, racism and many other issues. In striking contrast to its weakness at the large-scale level of doctrinal apologetics and politics, modern Christianity (mainline, not fundamentalist) is often very quick off the mark at the 'issues' or micro-power level.

In summary, we reject marxist optimism, scientism, essentialism and centralism; but we acknowledge the continuing influence of the marxist view of the self, society and history.

The question of art is more complex. Art in the West has often flowered in periods when an old order of things was exhausted and passing away, so that people could sense an opportunity to remake the world. Art does well in times of decay and rebirth, and there was a burst of creativity and excitement in Russia for a very few years after the October Revolution, before the dictators crushed it. The church needs something similar now, but it must be sustained. The Christian tradition that took shape in the Roman Empire has run its historical course and is in the very last stages of decadence and corruption. We have to make something new, and Christians need to become like artists. For the task ahead we need to develop emotional strength (for we are an effete lot) and a passionate love of freedom, doubt, dissent, heresy and creativity. At present we are slaves and mere ghosts of what we need to be. We should be libertarian to the point of anarchy, not because we are seeking to develop a unique extrasocial self, but because just now a hundred flowers must bloom. We are impoverished and starved of value. We've got to believe that we can improve upon what we have inherited. Passivity has been the order of the day in religion for so long that one must keep trumpetting that all our received forms of religious thought and moral practice were invented by human beings. They are now worn out and we can do better. We *have* to do better. We must invent a new world.

Notes

Introduction

1. The reason why art is central is that it was the first subject to go beyond the end of its own history and become Nietzschean and post-historical. The history of Western art was the history of a coherent international enterprise, of technical developments, and of a sustained struggle to achieve, in the work, both truth to Nature and the realization of the Platonic Idea of Beauty. Hegel presciently announced the end of that history, and modern art, boundlessly pluralistic and continually reinventing itself, has become something like a post-historical celebration of its own creativity in quest of itself. Marvellous: *and now other subjects have to follow*, especially religion and morality.

2. On the themes of these paragraphs, see my earlier works, *Life Lines* (1986) and *The Long-Legged Fly* (1987).

1. Christian Ethics as the Creation of Human Value

1. Enchiridion 75–77 (= Chapter XX in the Library of Christian Classics edition: A. C. Outler, *Augustine: Confessions and Enchiridion*, SCM Press 1955, pp.383–386).

2. The End of Two-Worlds Dualism

1. William Blake, the last stanza of *Auguries of Innocence*, from the Pickering manuscript; and *The Everlasting Gospel*, ll.71–74.

2. See Jacques Derrida's essay on Levinas in *Writing and Difference*, trans. Alan Bass, Routledge & Kegan Paul 1978, pp.79–153. In addition, it now seems to be established that late-ancient Jewish Apocalyptic thinking is just as much based on a two-worlds theory as is the thought of Plato himself.

3. K. E. Kirk, *The Vision of God*, Longmans 1931, pp.240, 237.

4. For a familiar English example see John Donne, *Holy Sonnets*XIV, 'Batter my heart . . .'

3. Ethics and the End of Philosophy

1. *Discourse on the Method* . . ., Part III.
2. See the opening of Michel Foucault, *Discipline and Punish*, trans. Alan Sheridan, Allen Lane 1977.
3. For these details, see the *Oxford English Dictionary* s.v.

4. Valuing our Values

1. For Foucault here, see his *History of Sexuality*, of course (especially Vol.2, *The Use of Pleasure*, introductory chapter 3); but see also the important later interview in Paul Rabinow (ed.), *The Foucault Reader*, Penguin Books 1986, pp.340 ff.; and the discussion by Arnold I. Davidson in David Couzens Hoy, (ed.), *Foucault: A Critical Reader*, Blackwell 1986, pp.221 ff.
2. *The Foucault Reader*, p.347.

5. Remaking the Christian Self

1. Anders Nygren, *Agape and Eros*, SPCK 1932–1939.
2. Robert Ornstein, *Multimind*, Macmillan 1986.
3. On all this, see Kant's essay, 'What is Enlightenment?' (1784).
4. Thomas J. J. Altizer, *History as Apocalypse*, State University of New York 1985, pp.27–29.
5. Schopenhauer's writings about death are the most interesting in the idealist tradition. See *The World as Will and Representation*, Vol.I, §54; Vol.II, c.XLI; *Parerga and Paralipomena*, Vol.II, Essay X. Use the E. J. Payne translations. Best summary: Brian Magee, *The Philosophy of Schopenhauer*, Oxford University Press 1983, pp.212–216.
6. On Paul's character as revealed in his text, see Graham Shaw, *The Cost of Authority*, SCM Press 1983.
7. The resignation of F. D. Maurice from his Chair in Theology at King's College, London in 1853 was one of the last great convulsions. Maurice's sin was to have appeared slightly to weaken the position of the ruling class, by casting some doubt upon the everlastingness of the torments of the damned.
8. Bernhard Lang, 'The Sexual Life of the Saints'; *Religion* 17, pp.149–171 (April 1987).
9. See Alan Keightley, *Into every life a little Zen must fall*, Wisdom Publications 1986.
10. Richard Harland, *Superstructuralism*, Methuen 1987, is perhaps the best one-volume introduction to recent French thought. Edward Craig, in *The Mind of God and the Works of Man*, Oxford University Press 1987, interestingly emphasizes the similarity between William James and Nietzsche. Like many recent writers,

Craig suggests that the implicit world-picture of Anglo-Saxon philosophy this century has not been so very different from the Continental
tradition as people used to think. See also *After Philosophy: End or
Transformation?* ed. Kenneth Baynes, James Bohman and Thomas
McCarthy, MIT Press 1987.

11. On Kierkegaard's relation to Feuerbach, see Alistair Hannay,
Kierkegaard, Routledge 1982, pp.174–77.

6. Remaking Christian Action

1. On the active and passive emotions see Spinoza's *Ethics*, Book III,
and studies by Stuart Hampshire and many others; and on active and
reactive forces in the personality see Gilles Deleuze, *Nietzsche and
Philosophy*, trans. Hugh Tomlinson, Athlone Press 1983, ch.2.

2. In the opening pages of this chapter I borrow some of Foucault's
ideas about bio-power. In the later pages I am at least partly indebted to
Wittgenstein.

3. Echoing the inscription on Kazantzakis' tomb in Crete.

4. See Peter Burke and Roy Porter (ed.), *The Social History of
Language*, Cambridge University Press 1987; a pioneering work.

5. Mary Douglas, *Natural Symbols* 2nd ed., Penguin 1973 etc.

6. See for example, John A .T. Robinson, *The Human Face of God*,
SCM Press 1973, pp.71 f., with notes 21, 22.

7. Explanations

1. 'Ethics' in the sense of Greek-type philosophical ethics, the
science of morals, is a term which has of course been in continuous use
since antiquity. But it really *does* need emphasizing that the term
'Christian ethics' is much less long-established. The earliest use cited in
the *OED* is 1855. We could improve on that by citing Thomas
Traherne's posthumously-published *Christian Ethicks* of 1675, but
Traherne's book is a mystical work and not quite about Christian
ethics in the modern sense.

2. For the phrase 'unlimited, unqualified individualism' see
E. Troeltsch, *The Social Teachings of the Christian Church*, trans. Olive
Wyon, Vol.1, Allen & Unwin 1931, p.55.

3. In his Introduction to Alan Keightley's book, *Into every life a little
Zen must fall*, cited above (Chapter 5, n.9), p.10.

4. Alasdair MacIntyre, *After Virtue*, Duckworth 1981, pp.244f.

8. Policies and Personalities

1. From the opening lines of the 1844 article, 'Towards a Critique of
Hegel's *Philosophy of Right*: An Introduction', especially: 'Man is no

abstract being, squatting outside the world. Man is the human world, the State, society.'

2. E.g., E. Kamenka, *Marxism and Ethics*, Routledge & Kegan Paul 1969.

Index of Names